Scrum

A Step by Step Pocket Guide to Make Twice the Work in Half the Time with Scrum

By

Alex Moore

© Copyright 2019 - All rights reserved.

The content contained within this book may not be reproduced, duplicated or transmitted without direct written permission from the author or the publisher.

Under no circumstances will any blame or legal responsibility be held against the publisher, or author, for any damages, reparation, or monetary loss due to the information contained within this book. Either directly or indirectly.

Legal Notice:

This book is copyright protected. This book is only for personal use. You cannot amend, distribute, sell, use, quote or paraphrase any part, or the content within this book, without the consent of the author or publisher.

Disclaimer Notice:

Please note the information contained within this document is for educational and entertainment purposes only. All effort has been executed to present accurate, up to date, and reliable, complete information. No warranties of any kind are declared or implied. Readers acknowledge that the author is not engaging in the rendering of legal, financial, medical or professional advice.

By reading this document, the reader agrees that under no circumstances is the author responsible for any losses, direct or indirect, which are incurred as a result of the use of information contained within this document, including, but not limited to, — errors, omissions, or inaccuracies.

Contents

Introduction 9
    Scrum: the Onetime revolutionary Strategy that Saves Nine .. 9

CHAPTER 1 11
    AGILE PROJECT MANAGEMENT 11
    What's need for Agile? 12
    Getting familiar with Agile Practice 14
    Benefits of Agile Processes 16

CHAPTER 2 20
    AGILE MANIFESTO 20
    What is Agile Manifesto? 20
    The aim of the Manifesto 21
    Four values of Agile Manifesto 22
    The 12 principles of Agile Manifesto 22

CHAPTER 3 29
    AGILE METHODOLOGIES 29
    Kanban Four Basic Operation Principles 32

Contrasting Kanban with Scrum Models 34

Why using RAD? 36

Seven principles of the Lean Framework 38

Benefits of the Lean Framework 38

CHAPTER 4 41

SPRINT AND SPRINT CYCLE 41

Sprint Cycle 42

CHAPTER 5 45

WHAT IS SCRUM? 45

Scrum versus Agile: Differences and Similarities 46

Benefits of Scrum method 49

CHAPTER 6 50

ANATOMY OF THE SCRUM FRAMEWORK 50

Scrum Rules 50

Scrum Rules versus Generally Accepted Scrum Practice (Non-Core Scrum Rules) 52

What is GASP or NCSR? 53

CHAPTER 7 55

USER STORIES AND CADENCE 55

Who writes user stories? 56

Tips to write excellent User Stories 57

Processes of a User Story 62

The INVEST criterion of User Story 64

CHAPTER 8 67

SCRUM FLOW 67

Scrum Process Flow 69

Scrum tasks 71

How to create and add Task.. 72

Eight Steps to a complete Scrum Process Flow 73

CHAPTER 9 76

SCRUM BURN DOWN AND VELOCITY 76

Purpose of the Velocity 79

How to calculate Velocity in a sprint 79

Differences between the velocity chart and burn down chart 82

CHAPTER 10 86

SCRUM ARTIFACTS... 86

The Product Backlog 87

Scrum Focus Areas... 95

CHAPTER 11 98

SCRUM CEREMONIES 98

1. Sprint Planning 100

2. Daily Scrum 100

    3. Sprint Review 100

    4. Sprint Retrospective... 100

CHAPTER 12 111

    THE SCRUM CORE AND NON-CORE ROLES 111

CHAPTER 13 119

    SCALING SCRUM 119

Chapter 14...125

    CONCLUSION...125

Introduction

Scrum: the Onetime revolutionary Strategy that Saves Nine

Jakes started an IT firm two and a half years ago, but the experience almost turned sour and the thought regrettable after the managers were unable to understand the tricks of harnessing the human capital and resources available at their disposal. In a bid to reinvent the company and make the initial vision that drove the project work, the naive Board fired and hired new brains and invested fresh funds.

However, despite the novel ideas and resources brought on, things got worse. Then Jakes wanted to quit but his ambitious mind kept spurring him to reengage the process and bring strategies that might change the dwindling fortune of things.

"What is going on," furious Jakes demanded in one of the meetings with the other members of the board.

"I think we keep hiring professional and experts who work at crossroads in terms of vision and purpose," Stems responded in a rather bold-faced manner.

"Mr Stems, what do you insinuate," Jakes queried.

"Or perhaps he's suggesting there is lack of team work and that employees despite all their expertise, tested experience and in-depth skills aren't working with unity of purpose, Nathan cut in.

"Exactly my point, engineer Nathan, Stems quickly responded. "Clearly, there is lack of team work."

Surprisingly, few months down the line, Dan, an outsource expert in company analysis and project management, sought to help Jakes and his team solve the puzzle. Dan had engaged a new invention called 'Scrum' in his previous projects for many of his numerous clients.

So, he introduced the book "Scrum: The Art of Doing Twice the Work in Half the Time" to Jakes' company and by dint of some miracle, the entire IT firm recorded a huge turnaround. And now, it is competing at the top level with the best 20 IT firms in the region.

CHAPTER 1

AGILE PROJECT MANAGEMENT

Perhaps, the best way to start is to say that you've got to stay agile. Yes, you have to. To be agile means to be active, vibrant, and productive. So, when you first heard the word 'Agile' during your first session in business management and software development conference, what was your first reaction like? Confusion? Bewilderment? Something related to your old school days psychology? I guess, you're not alone in the plane of confusion and guesses.

Guess what? Agile is actually a project management software that seeks to help companies achieve more target within a pretty short time. You must be familiar with the biblical Israelites who wasted so much precious and invaluable number of years traversing from Egypt to the Canaan Land. Historians told us the wandering Israelites spent approximately 40 years for a journey that normally should have taken them 40 days. That's crazily unnecessary? Maybe, that for you is a story that best passes for a myth.

In our ever changing world influenced by the impact of technology, there are quite a number of issues that the corporate environment faces which make it increasingly difficult to vouch for customers' loyalty, address support issues, meet clients' needs or achieve project goals and requirements within timeframe.

Historically, companies have been dynamic in their approach, the drive to keep traditional business processes has been challenged with the evanescent nature of the technology-driven business ecosystem.

Not only that the traditional processes are not fast enough, their complexity and sophistication to deal with emerging issues is quite insignificant. Yet, companies have to respond adequately to the needs of the clients.

Hence, these challenges and the necessity of meeting these needs have given rise to technology experts, focused on project management, product management and software development, to build Agile, a new software development process and models of doing things. Differently.

Responsiveness needs have forced from obscurity and nonexistence the evolution of agile and more efficient tools that would not only improve on traditional Waterfall methodologies but also, and more importantly upstage them in the final analysis.

What's need for Agile?

Many project management and software development enthusiasts have asked the usual question any local would ask when a new sheriff enters the town. The question that has surfaced is: why the need for Agile, after all the beautiful functionality and features our traditional Waterfall offers? If the process I'm currently adopting is working perfectly for me, why transition to new model?

But change is the only thing that is constant and you can be sure that every upgrade on an existing model especially in the IT world is always a disruptive one. Imagine the period Windows XP, Linux and Windows 7 were in vogue and compare the functions and features of Windows 8 and 10 to them. The two cycles are world apart, no doubt.

So, the area of product development and management is no different. The product development that was acceptable some ten years ago could no longer be used for the dynamism that changes have brought.

No doubt, what you consider as first rate yesterday can no longer pass that test today. Ditto, what's today's "fast enough" would not be fast enough for tomorrow's needs and changing requirements.

The greatest benefit of the Agile technology is to put companies at that competitive edge where they can deploy the Agile processes to help the keep up with the accelerating rate of change.

With Agile process, software companies can develop software quicker and at lower costs relative to what is obtainable using the Waterfall. Hence, Agile gives software developers a competitive advantage in a fast-paced market. That sounds theoretical and abstract. Ok, let's get to the benefits of Agile in concrete terms.

As an upgrade over Waterfall, Agile does not require much or in-depth planning at the initial stage of a project. At every stage, Agile practices and methodologies are open to changes based on feedback from end users.

Agile is to be thought of in terms of a familiar process that is, a series of small waterfalls that have very quick iterations and give fast responsiveness ratio. Agile teams are multi and cross-functional and can work on iterations of a product for a time.

Using Agile, you are able to organize all delivered tasks into a backlog. Work iterations are set in relation to the work value relative to the needs and aspirations of the customer and business. At the end each iteration, the product is always work in progress.

However, prioritization of needs and projects as well as alignment of needs of customers and business is an important job that business stakeholders and developers should sit down and work out.

Getting familiar with Agile Practice

So, what is Agile? By simple definition Agile is a software development process. Agile is an incremental, iterative approach to software development.

As a process, Agile is used to describe an approach of managing projects and general attitude to software development.

Interestingly, Agile development has its origins and usage in technology rather than in science. In other words, the method is rooted in practice than academia.

Agile practices and processes are best used both in software development and also in all functional areas of the organizational life. This is why leadership in Agile methodologies encourages teamwork, close customer collaboration, frequent and prompt deliveries of working tools, direct communication, accountability, and ability to respond to change.

Agile was originally develop to give a more change responsive process leaders and software developers. Hence, with Agile, industry managers and IT experts can respond to changes and changing requirements with the process rolling out needed functionality.

Besides, in mind for developing Agile framework and making it an advanced model over Waterfall is the need to respond to a number of questions which businesses and software developers seek to find answer to. Some of those questions include:

- What should good Agile practitioners and teams know and do?
- How do we train developers and teams to become good Agile-compliant users?
- How do we transition from plan-driven Waterfall development to practice-oriented Agile development?

- What available tools to practice Agile development?
- How are those tools to be used to give support to Agile practices?
- How can businesses and companies do to manage projects using various Agile practices and frameworks?
- How can companies, organizational processes, and industry develop an efficiency model that would help towards achieving team-targeted rather than individual member-inclined teamwork?
- How do industries define their task job in terms of the client's mission?
- How should software companies not define their jobs as analysts, designers, programmers, testers, or project managers?

Benefits of Agile Processes

Allows for flexible change

While there is focus on value, change becomes investable to processes. Agile processes allow for real change during iteration. Items on Product Backlog can always be reprioritized and refined to meet the need that is urgent. The team has more control in managing and customizing the Product Backlog, review processes and view project progress. The work needs to be shipped early to get expected Return on investment.

Predictable Costs and Schedule

The fixed nature of the Sprint gives the team a sense of predictability in terms of cost, schedule and result of the work done. The team is able to combine estimated costs before each Sprint, giving the client a sense of what it would cost them to have their project done by the team. In this way, there is seamless and more improved decision-making opportunities and prioritizing on the part of both the team and the client.

It facilitates Transparency

The agile approach actively engages the client from the project's start to finish. The processes involve the clients right the blast of whistle at the iteration planning stage through review sessions, up till new feature builds in the software. Clients are able to see and follow up on a project all through stages and not until the final end of the project. That in itself encourages transparency and all-party involvement.

Focuses on Value

Agile provides the platform for the team to focus on value their software brings to business table. They focus on answering questions: What does the client need? How do we help the business to grow? How does our software help deliver features that give the most value to client's business?

User-focused

Agile processes define product features and descriptions as they help business growth and product acceptance using the user's stories. Focusing on the user's needs and expectations helps the team to deliver real value and not building an IT project for consumers.

During each process, Agile processes give opportunity for users and consumers to evaluate and give feedback to the developers and team through testing after each Sprint.

Improves Quality

Agile encourages projects to be broken into handy units in order to ease the burden of heavy task for the team. The focus is to enhance quality and prompt delivery of development. In that way, project testing and team collaboration become seamless. By creating smaller teams that focus on different part of project, the results become more qualitative. N that way, too, conducting tests reviews throughout the iteration, defects and mismatches can easily be spotted and fixed.

It sets purpose for your team

Agile methodologies focus on creating a value-added and shared sense of ownership and objectives for all team members. Put differently, every member of the team is an owner of the project. What this does is that it gives your team a sense of belonging and purpose rather than creating a false sense of urgency. Interestingly, purposeful teams achieve more and are more productive and efficient than a pack of individuals with no synergy.

CHAPTER 2

AGILE MANIFESTO

Every project as it were is driven by certain core values and short, medium and long-term plans. These values consist of the guiding principles that should inform the actions and tasks of creators and innovators of designs and inventions in any field.

Authors of the Agile project also believe that there are certain ethics and principles which should guide the works and operations of software developers. Harnessing these values help software developers build trust with team and clients, and confidence and competence in themselves.

What is Agile Manifesto?

Agile Manifesto therefore refers to a declaration which expresses four core values and 12 principles software developers can use to grow competence and develop quality IT service to clients.

The understanding is that proper management and maintenance of excellent relationship with clients goes beyond possession of skills and expertise. Agile authors also believe that it is not just sufficient to procure standard IT contract negotiations. There are best practices that can effectively help software developers maximize quality service delivery, especially in an environment where there are multiple service providers in the IT industry.

The manifesto contains four key values and 12 principles. Each of the section provides software developers with new insight into decentralizing the heavy processes that hitherto define software development.

The aim of the Manifesto

The aim of the manifesto, among other things, is to overhaul the entire process of software development. For them, the processes of developing software over the years have been encumbered with a lot of bureaucracy. The processes, too, are unresponsive and uni-dimensional in terms of documentation requirements.

The four key values outlined in the Agile Manifesto seek to promote process in software development that focuses on quality through creation of products that meet the needs and expectations of consumers.

In the same vein, the 12 principles are intended to fashion and backing a software development work environment which targets the customer. In that process, the principles will create an environment that relates to business goals and objectives, no less responding and pivoting quickly to changes and feedbacks from the point of view of the end users.

Hence, the manifesto is seeking to maintain a balance and restore credibility to the word of methodology. The implementation of the Agile manifesto, the authors believe, would be not only to plan but also recognize the limit of planning in an ever changing digital ecosystem.

Furthermore, the authors focus on a software development approach that is committed to creating software incrementally. The approach will in a way provide Agile users with new versions, or releases of software following brief sprints.

Four values of Agile Manifesto

The Agile Manifesto declares four core values of Agile software development. They include:

- Individuals and interactions over processes and tools
- Working software over comprehensive documentation;
- Customer collaboration over contract negotiation; and
- Responding to change over following a plan.

The 12 principles of Agile Manifesto

The 12 principles declared in the Agile Manifesto include:

1. Customer Satisfaction

The Agile methodologies are designed to meet the needs and expectations of customers through early and continuous delivery of valuable work. It is believed that software developers can only earn trust of customers through prompt and resilient prioritization of their needs.

2. Keeping sizeable workload

The Agile methodologies consider breaking down big task into smaller manageable units that can be completed quickly. Simplicity is the watchword for the Agile Manifesto.

Essentially, all Agile methodologies require the art of maximizing the amount of work not done. They ruthlessly focus on cutting down functionality that does not lend value to the chin process.

3. Self-structured team

Agile recognizes that having the best works, architectures, designs, and delivery requires that the team is properly organized. However, a team does not get structured from without; it has to self-motivate and self-organize in order to deliver best solution.

In that process, a self-organized team becomes cross and multi-functional, identifying potential threats and project issues even before they constitute real impediments to the project.

4. Welcoming Change Requirements

Software developers can be more productive and responsive to customers' needs only if they recognize the necessity of welcoming change, even late in developmental stages of the project. Agile processes and methodologies are designed in such a way that they welcome changing requirements.

The change however, should be harnessed towards customer's competitive advantage. The Agile project discourages despair in the face of change, however tough the changing requirements could present themselves to the developer or project manager.

Reacting to change as fast and excellent as possible gives the developer a leverage to get closer to client's needs, and it is a good signpost of progress.

5. Sustainable Effort

Creating processes that promote and support sustainable efforts and collective development is very essential to fashioning a balanced working environment, and Agile processes and methodologies identify and promote that initiative.

Ideally, Agile is designed in such that it encourages that every member in the chain process- sponsors, developers and end users- should be able to work at constant pace and maintain that indefinitely.

The slogan, 'think, work, and balance' quite fits into the proposal of a sustainable effort. Everyone should deeply be involved in getting the project to its final lap. In this way, there would be quality work done in the same degree that the team is also qualitatively impacted.

Agile strives to maintain a consistent level of activity among members in the chain process. The consistency will translate to a better ability to forecast.

6. Measuring progress

What about measuring progress by the amount of completed work? This is a key aspect of the Agile methodologies. Developing software is one of the key factors in measuring work progress.

The objective of the goal must take precedence over religious following of plan. This is so because the more involved you get in following plans, the more distracted you get away from the real goal of the project.

Agile deemphasizes constant documentation update that does not result from measuring progress but strict obedience to plans.

7. Value-added and update-driven solution

As far as Agile is concerned, technical excellence and good design enhance agility. Hence, it is important to pay close attention to this aspect of the project.

The solution derived from a beautiful design is more valuable and meaningful than having an elegant design that does give a result that will stand the test of time.

Agile processes also believes that what is more so is the solution that is capable and open to constant update that will keep it in the loop of currency.

An elegant design, in Agile reckoning must not only be solution provider but also and more importantly delivers a solution that can maintain its value through update and maintenance cycles.

8. Frequent and fast project Delivery

Agile methodologies focus on delivering frequently. The idea is that frequent delivery of working software helps developers to get faster feedback from end uses. The developers will in turn be able to quickly identify what needs to be changed.

The sooner a developer delivers incremental software, the better for the team. Preference to shorter timescale is fundamental to help spot a wrong turn in the process of developing or communicating with the client.

It would be better in Agile mechanism to find out earlier where an errors lies and promptly fix it than having a complete work required for rework.

9. Working through the project

Project managers and software developers must work together on the project throughout the entire process. Also, it is not out of place to have the customer take part in the process of project delivery.

Working through the project consists in understanding that both the customer and the developer are geared towards achieving the same goal.

10. Direct Conversation

Adopting face-to-face mechanism in the process of communication among team members is as crucial as the overall goal of the team. Team performs most efficiently and effectively if they are able of inculcate the method of conveying information face-to-face.

While being in the same location may be ideal and encouraged, having an osmotic sort of communication where co-location is impossible, can also effectively deliver the same result, if handled properly.

Team leaders must keep everyone in the loop of development via direct communication. Using a third party to deliver message may hamper the entire process and so defeat the goal of the team. It is important therefore to improve the technical aspect of communication techniques among team.

11. Motivating Team Members

Individuals in a team want to build projects. They want to be part of the trusted with projects. Software developers and project managers must motivate individual team members by providing them with excellent environment that supports them.

Agile processes and methodologies emphasize self-organizing teams who impulsively and without compulsion are able to manage both themselves and the work. The need for a micromanagement of projects may no longer be required.

12. Use After Action Review for Effectiveness

Reflection is one key the Agile Manifesto also declares as one principle that delivers incredible outcome and synergizes team.

At regular intervals, team members must meet to deliberate on how they can become more efficient.

It is in the process they can inject new ideas, tune and adjust members' behaviours. The use of After-Action Review helps you improve on the next project for the next client. And it is important to review previously finished projects in order to deliver a better one in the future.

Agile projects come with several ceremonies, among which is the Retrospective. At the end of each Sprint or Iteration, Agile encourages that teams should meet in order to catch and improve behaviors before they start a new project.

Not carrying out the review portends a grave danger and detrimental impact on the project. Since agile is based on transparency, technical excellence, respect, trust and commitment, creating high-performing teams helps value individuals and interactions over processes and tools.

CHAPTER 3

AGILE METHODOLOGIES

Agile methodologies refer to the different models and mechanisms in which the Agile practice can be implemented. The type of methodology to be used depends on the project the team wants to work on.

There are several different frameworks used to execute Agile process. While they take their inspiration and mechanism from the same Agile source, each of the methodologies differ slightly in the manner they are implemented. These include:

1. **Extreme programming**

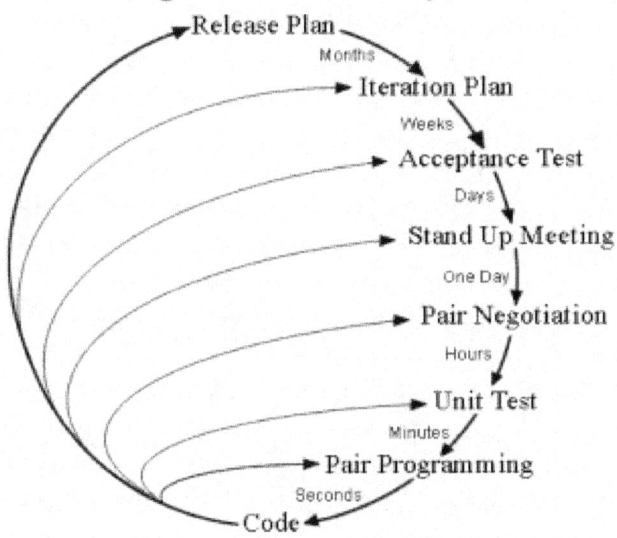

This is one of the methodologies used to implement Agile practice. It is a software development and project management method that intends to enhance quality and responsiveness to change and changing requirements.

It also refers to that agile development methodology that is deployed in software development which allows programmers and software developers to make decisions on the scope of deliveries.

Extreme Programming (XP) remains one of the most popular and yet controversial agile frameworks. For software developers looking to continually and quickly deliver software of high quality, then this highly disciplined methodology is the best o use.

One of its features is that Extreme Programming encourages customer participation and each one is involved with the closely knitted team from the planning stage.

The methodology of Extreme Programming operates on four key principles:

1. Simplicity
2. Communication
3. Feedback
4. Courage

In addition to these values, the framework also has 12 backup practices:

1. Plan the game
2. Make releases in small milestones
3. Take customer acceptance tests
4. Make design simple
5. Execute programming in pairs
6. Development should be driven by test
7. Feature again and again
8. Make integration continuous
9. Team ownership of code
10. Set standards for coding
11. Representation
12. Keep workable working speed

2. Kanban

Kanban is framework that operates on the principle of visual implementation of Agile. It is a technique for managing work, with a highlight on just-in-time delivery. Associated with the Kanban framework is the Kanban Board.

The Kanban board refers to a work and workflow visualisation device which provides a summary of the status, progress, and issues related to the work. This model of agile execution encourages mini and unbroken changes to the related system.

Kanban framework operates on the following principles:

- Visual workflow
- Restricting work-in-progress
- Enhancement and management of workflow
- Making explicit policies
- Continuous improvement

Kanban Four Basic Operation Principles

Kanban operates on four basic principles:

1. No setup, no procedure

That sounds raw! That is exactly what it is. Like much of what defines Agile project, Kanban does not have a preset set nor does it prescribe a certain procedure. The framework allows the team to start with it has now; you can always overlay Kanban properties over existing workflow. In this way, you can bring in change.

2. Be ruthless with incremental not sweeping change

Kanban operates with an ideal that suggests accord with incremental, evolutionary change. Since the framework is designed to meet minimal opposition, it encourages continuous incremental and evolutionary changes to your current system. The framework does not encourage sweeping changes because of great resistance capacity.

3. Focus on existing process and role

The Kanban design is one which recognizes that the existing roles, process and responsibilities have values in themselves. Hence, Kanban doesn't prohibit process; it doesn't prescribe either. Existing process can yield you desired result and generate broader support for your Kanban implementation. But a sudden change can alter setup and progress.

4. Leadership must show at all levels

This principle is not an exclusive operational procedure of the Kanban methodology. Many Agile methodologies including Scrum, RAD also adopt it. It doesn't matter which part of the ladder rung you belong, you should act leadership.

Put simply, you don't have to be a team or executive before you play that leadership role. If you occupy the frontline any team, you are expected to act that quality. Endeavor to show character trait that fosters team spirit and a mindset that encourages continual enhancement to reach team goal.

Contrasting Kanban with Scrum Models

Kanban shares some indistinguishable similarities with the Scrum framework. However, the two have some differences which should not be confused with each other.

	Scrum	Kanban
Cadence	Regular fixed length sprints (that is, 2 weeks)	Continuous flow
Method of Release	At the end of each sprint depending on whether or not the product owner approves it	Continuous delivery or at the team's discretion
Roles	Product owner, scrum master, scrum development team	No existing roles. Some teams enlist the help of an agile coach
Key metrics	Velocity	Cycle time
Change process	Teams should strive to not make changes to the sprint forecast during the sprint.	Change can happen at any time during sprint

	Any change can potentially compromise learnings	

3. Rapid Application Development (RAD)

This is one Agile Development methodology which enables software developers and programmers to build solutions with the speed of light by talking directly to end users to meet business requirement.

In simple terms, RAD is less talk, more action because it de-emphasizes strict planning. Although the methodology stresses action over plan, using RAD requires that the developer still takes some steps through the development. The steps in order are figure out requirements, build prototypes, get user feedback, build again, test, and implement.

RAD is cool with your team especially when you need to get some project done quickly. It delivers a working system more quickly than a traditional technique such as Waterfall would do. Also make use of RAD only when you have the budget. This is because it requires you to have a team of highly professional and skilled developers. And you know they would demand some cool cash. Thirdly, you can use Rapid application development when you have an available pool of users and clients who ca reliably test you prototypes.

Why using RAD?

Some of the advantages of using RAD to build your software include that you get a working product more quickly. By that we mean that you can present your work-in-progress in piecemeal allowing your team to put them all together at the end of the whole process.

Also, using allows you to get direct and constant feedback from user. Since you can show your user or client your work in progress, they send to you what you need to remove, add or adjust. You can get their feedback directly and as quick as you want them. That gives you opportunity to improve on your work and implementation becomes easier.

Furthermore, using RAD gives you the latitude to break a large project into smaller units and tasks. There are two things opportunities this offers you. One, when developing a large application, breaking it into smaller unites allows you to form a more specialized team of developers who concentrate on a certain area of the project. The second advantage flows from the first: you can create small wins for your team, allowing you to motivate them. In that way, you have more hands-on deck to help through then entire project.

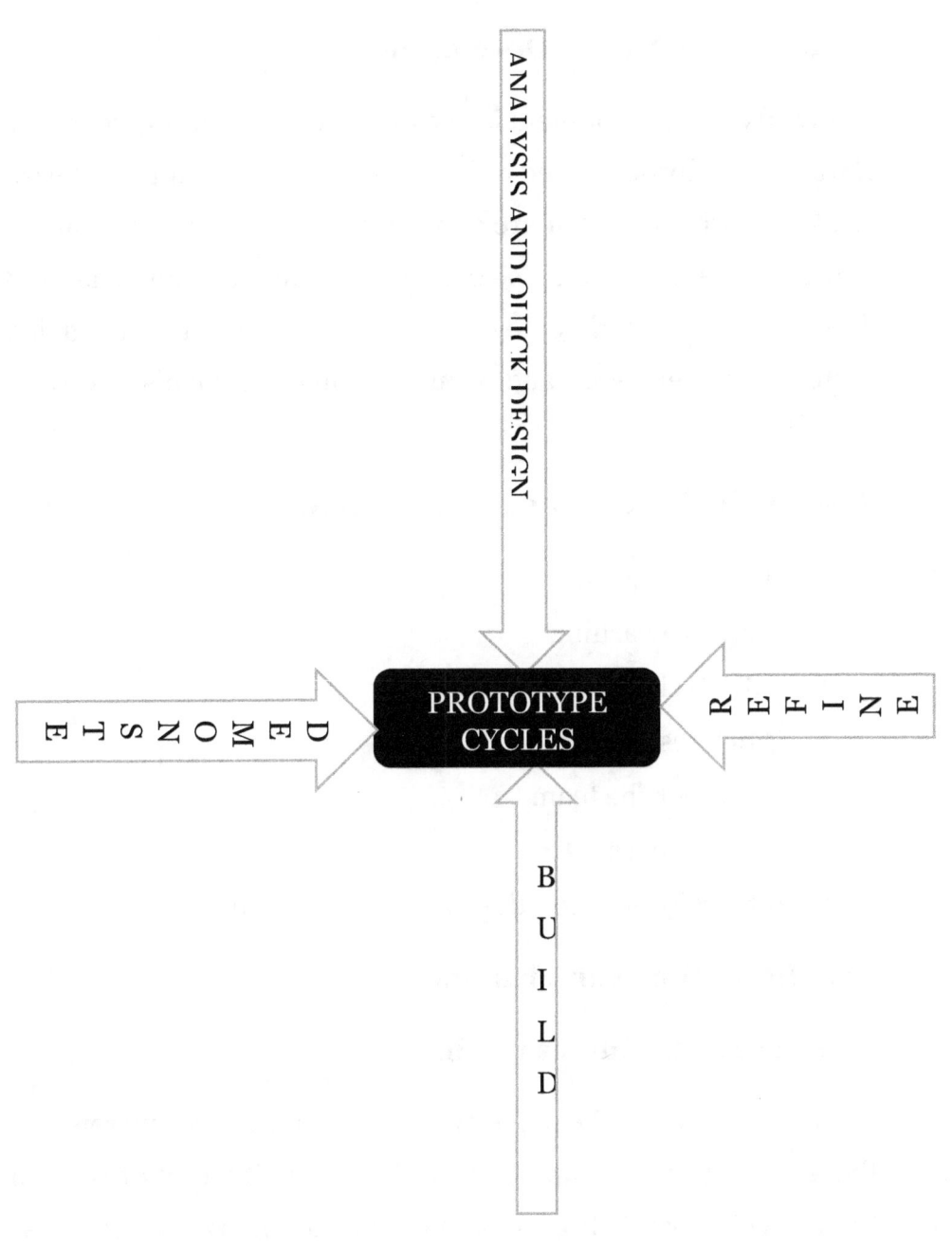

4. Lean Software Development

Lean software development is one of the Agile iteration processes. It was originally developed by Mary and Tom Poppendieck. Learn is a set of principles that are applicable to software development in order to reduce stress on cost, programming, mismatches and defect rates. The methodology focuses on adding value and giving customer an efficient and value-oriented mechanism t their project.

Seven principles of the Lean Framework

- Waste Removal
- Amplify Learning
- Late Decision Making
- Quick result Delivery
- Empower the team
- Build Integrity
- Integrally envision the whole Application

Benefits of the Lean Framework

1. Lean eliminates roadblocks

In the context of the Learn software development, waste refers to the anything that is capable of reducing the quality of code or hindering time and effort to be spent on coding. Waste could also be defined as any the roadblock to business value deliverables. Example of such bottlenecks include unnecessary code or functionality, delays in programming, blurred requirements, and insufficient testing.

2. Provides customer needs at less cost

The focus of Lean methodology there is to eliminate these hindrances, adopting requisite technologies, and gaining insight into what the customer really needs and expects. One other advantage of the lean framework is that customers can make late but informed decision thus reducing the cost of their investment on the project.

3. Enhances business value

As an iterative development framework, Lean is poised to deliver new applications for enhancements in a quick and smart way. Thus, integrity is built into it to make ensure seamless flow of architecture and system components.

4. Easy to Incorporate

Lean principle also gives organizations the leverage to integrate and achieve continuous improvement as they rapidly introduce and implement changes in their system.

5. Crystal

Crystal Agile framework is one methodology in the development of software that is both lightweight and adaptable. As an approach, Crystal features several agile processes including Clear,

Crystal Yellow, Crystal Orange, and other unique methods characteristic of Agile.

There are several factors that drive Crystal processes, which include the size of the team, the criticality of the system, and the priorities of the project the team is undertaking. Crystal method operates with the principle that each project is unique in its own right. Correspondingly, too, the policies and practices that would guide their implementation must also be tailored to their specific requirements and features to be able to meet the need of the customer.

Crystal, like most of the Agile processes, also operates with its unique tenets and principles. In addition to these tenets, Crystal focuses on promoting early and frequent working software releases. Besides, this Agile process also encourages high user engagement, builds adaptability and eliminates distractions and stifling bureaucracy

Crystal principles are:

- Teamwork
- Communication
- Simplicity
- Reflection
- Frequent adjustments
- Improved processes

CHAPTER 4

SPRINT AND SPRINT CYCLE

What is Sprint?

Scrum sprint is a term associated with and used mainly in Agile methodology. It refers to one time-boxed iteration of a continuous cycle in a scrum development. Within a sprint, a team plans, designs and defines the amount of work it wants to complete and made ready for review. In a short common meaning, especially as used in athletics, Sprint could mean a short race at full speed.

Development Teams define a short duration of a sprint, usually between 2 to 4 weeks. Scrum Sprint requires that the team collectively sets the target (technically referred to as Sprint Goal) they want to meet and this is always done in collaboration with the Product Owner. The work plan is itemized in order of priority in the Sprint backlog during Sprint Planning session.

Once the team starts the scrum sprint, team works together to complete planned work effectively and make it ready for review by Product Owner, Scrum Master, stakeholders, customers, end users, among others, by the end of that period.

Before starting a Sprint cycle, a team is expected and mandatorily required to have readied high level User Stories in Product backlog. With the help of Sprint Analytics, Scrum Master and

Product Owner can monitor the progress of team work in Sprint in one full glance. The Sprint Analytics helps the Development team, Scrum Master and product Owner to define Sprint Goal and analyze the work done within each Sprint.

The figure below shows an overview of Scrum Flow for one Sprint:

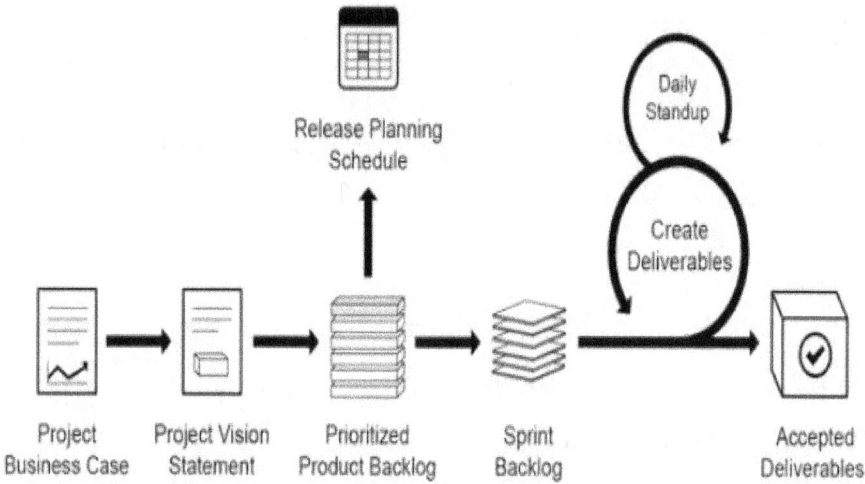

Sprint Cycle

Each Sprint starts with a Sprint Planning Meeting. It is at this coming –together the team considers including high priority User Stories in the Sprint. Generally, a Sprint does not last more than between one and six weeks. During this period, the Scrum Team works on generating potentially shippable Deliverables or product increments.

While the Sprint is underway, the team (which include the Product Owner, Scrum Master, Development Team and stakeholders) also conducts short, highly focused Daily Standup Meetings. This is where team members deliberate on daily progress.

Again, towards the end of the Sprint, the team conducts a Sprint Review as a way of getting stakeholders involved. At this Review, the Scrum Development Team provides demonstrable deliverables of the project they have worked on to the Product Owner and relevant stakeholders.

The purpose of the Review is to have their feedback and remarks on the projects. The Product Owner accepts the Deliverables only if they meet the predefined Acceptance Criteria and Project Requirements. However, the project is rejected and the team is asked to go and rework it to meet the expectations.

After the Review, the Development Team conducts what is called the Sprint Retrospect Meeting where members discuss ways to improve processes and performance in order to deliver better result that they would demonstrate to the rest of the team in the next Sprint Review.

Is there a difference between Sprint and Iteration?

This is one question that a lot of new initiates into the Agile process often like to ask. Especially with the changing trends and advancing technologies, mobile and web applications developers are finding it hard and sometimes difficult to adopt to this changes ad advancements. Other similar include is Sprint just another term for Iteration? Can we have Sprints within Iterations or Iterations within Sprints? What is the interim release to a client before the planned Sprint release data called?

An iteration is the umbrella agile term used for a single development cycle. It is often a commonly used in the IID, that is, Iterative and Incremental Development. Scrum, on the other hand, is a specialized agile framework or a specialized Incremental Development process which uses the Sprint to represent its iterations. In other words, o e development cycle in Scrum is called a Sprint.

Every Agile methodology has a name for its iteration. So, Sprint is Scrum specific. Sprint is an iteration. However, an iteration in Extreme programming or Crystal or EED, etc, are not Sprints.

CHAPTER 5

WHAT IS SCRUM?

Getting familiar with Scrum

Looking to build a fast-moving, cross-functional team and engage every member that makes up your team work to achieve set goal, then Scrum is for you. Scrum is not designed to focus on individual member of a team.

Rather, it focuses on the team and how to harness their potentials to meet target. Like Jakes and his firm, making people get to work together to get things done in a more agile and efficient way is the way to go.

Scrum can simply be defined as the agile and efficient way to execute and manage a project, especially software development. As one of the process enhancement strategies in agile (we shall discuss agile shortly) and development rather than a methodology, Scrum is better viewed as a framework for managing processes. Scrum is an invention, a framework that helps team synergizes and works together.

Scrum refers to an iterative and incremental framework useful for managing product development. Scrum defines a flexible, full product development approach where a development team works closely and collectively to achieve a common target.

The framework allows and enables teams to self-organize by encouraging physical co-location or synergize knitted online collaboration of all team members, as well as daily face-to-face communication among all team members involved.

This brilliant, discursive, thought-provoking book is setting the tune for leadership and management process across various industries. The invention is practically changing not only the way we relate as co-workers, but also influencing our way of life and thought process.

It was clear from our pathetic story that the focus for Jakes and his team, over the years, should not have been on firing, hiring and headhunting. Energy should have been channeled towards making the management and top hierarchy bring together the various expertise and skills to bear on the company.

Scrum versus Agile: Differences and Similarities

One term closely associated with Scrum is Agile. We have discussed this extensively in our first chapter, but it is important we compare and contrast it with Scrum, one of its 'offspring's'. From the word go, you understand agile to be the umbrella term that consists of all methods and approaches that bring about change in the Development Team' process.

Let us see the relationship between Scrum and agile in this way: your kitchen's Dishwasher got spoilt by the high energy supply and you need to change it. You go to an electronic store where you see various models and brands of TVs.

There you see Samsung, Panasonic, Frigidaire, LG, Hisense, Tecno, Bosch and so on. Eventually, you settle for and leave the store with say a Bosch, perhaps because you think it has strong resistance to high voltage. That's exactly the same way Scrum relates to agile. Consider agile as the dishwasher, while Scrum is your preferred Bosch, one of the dishwasher brands.

But here is the contrast: while you may not be able to customize your dishwasher, agile processes, like Scrum, can be made to suit your needs. In that case, you can integrate other desirable features you find in other agile processes into Scrum.

For instance, you could employ components of Extreme programming, let's say test-driven development and pair programming into Scrum processes. That is the sort of flexibility and personalization feature that comes with agile. The flexibility of the agile process is one of those features that appeal to its numerous users.

Scrum is one of the many agile processes which also feature others like Extreme Programming, Adaptive System Development, DSDM, Feature Driven Development, Kanban, Crystal and more.

Agile means change, and it represents an umbrella name for all activities and approaches in software development. It is a term used to describe a general methodology used to achieve software development. Each of the agile methods, including Scrum, focuses on:

1. Teamwork
2. Frequent deliveries of working software
3. Close customer collaboration
4. Ability to respond quickly to change.

One of the key selling point of the agile processes is that it cuts a larger software project into several manageable breakdowns. Hence, it allows for the development team to handle projects in increments and iterations.

This is the point that separates the Agile management approach from other management systems. Agile like Scrum management, uses iterations at every phase of software development.

Agile process work with the proven results from studies that larger chunk of work does not most time yield expected result. Besides, studies have shown that the shorter a project, the higher its success rate.

The agile approach is to reduce as much as possible the size of the project in order to fashion out as many several smaller projects from it as possible. This will help the teams to manage and finish iteration easily.

Benefits of Scrum method

While it may be difficult to switch from say Crystal to DSDM or any other agile approaches, it is so easy using Scrum. Adopting the Scrum process has some positive feedbacks that apparently set it ahead of other agile processes. The benefits of using the Scrum frameworko are related and they build into each other. They include:

- Higher productivity
- Higher quality
- Reduced time-to-market
- Improved stakeholder satisfaction
- Increased job satisfaction
- More engaged employees

CHAPTER 6

ANATOMY OF THE SCRUM FRAMEWORK

What do you have to look out for as Scrum features?

The Scrum framework consists of a number of components that every leader needs to pay close attention to. Each part is integral to the overall functionality of the system to your company growth and process improvement. Besides, each module is integrated into the framework to serve a specific purpose and functions for the overall applicability and usage of the framework.

The Scrum framework is a merger of what is called Scrum Teams. The Teams have as their members associated roles, events, artifacts, and rules. Integrally, the rules are the bridges that connects the roles, events, and artifacts together. The rules serve as the guides, while if violated may lead to disruption of process and patchy operation and usage of the entire system and impact of constituent members. We shall now discuss each of these components.

Scrum Rules

Here are rules save you time, money and resources. The Scrum framework consists of basic frequently mentioned rules that guide the usage of the framework. As earlier noted, the rules are bridges that bind all other constituent members of the whole framework together. The rules clutch the Scrum process together so that everyone knows how to play and adhere.

Take the foundation away, the entire building collapses; remove the bridge, interconnectivity and communications break and chaos takes over. If you understand the meaning and purpose of chain action, then you appreciate how crucial the roles of the rules in the entire Scrum schematics.

Here is the great piece of news that may interest leaders who want to adopt the Scrum framework. And there is no reason why management should not adopt it. Interestingly, The Scrum system has the Scrum Master which helps in ensuring that everyone in the team follows the rules of Scrum as they relate to a specific project.

The main purpose of the Scrum rules is to achieve efficiency. Rules are set in the framework to ensure process improvement, optimize development systems, minimize waste, and effectively make use of scarce time and resources. Below is a list of basic rules in the Scrum model:

1. Every Sprint is Four Weeks or Less in Duration
2. There are no Breaks Between Sprints
3. Every Sprint is the Same Length
4. The Intention of Every Sprint is "Potentially Shippable" Software
5. Every Sprint includes Sprint Planning

6. The Sprint Planning Meeting is Time boxed to 2 Hours / Week of Sprint Length
7. The Daily Scrum occurs every day at the same time of day
8. The Daily Scrum is time boxed to 15 minutes
9. Every Sprint includes Sprint review for stakeholder feedback on the product
10. Every Sprint includes Sprint Retrospective for the team to inspect and adapt
11. Review and Retrospective meetings are time boxed in total to 2 hours / week of Sprint length
12. There is no break between Sprint Review and Retrospective meetings

Scrum Rules versus Generally Accepted Scrum Practice (Non-Core Scrum Rules)

Note must be taken not to confuse the Scrum rules with what could simply be regarded as the Generally Accepted Scrum Practices, abbreviated as GASP. It could also be regarded as the Non-Core Scrum Rules (NCSR).

While a Scrum rule is an inviolable process that if a team fails to do, they aren't doing Scrum, a GASP is some activity that sufficient number of Scrum teams are doing. We shall present that shortly in a table form. That would guide us when using the framework.

But we shall first and foremost define, in a formal style, what we mean by GASP or NCSR. Here's a working definition we can use.

Besides, conducting a review meeting of a sprint at the end of the sprint is a GASP or NCSR and not a Scrum rule. Yet, a tea would still be considered to be doing scrum even if they overlook a sprint review meeting. There are teams who enjoy as common practice an after-sprint mini review rather than involving in a serious and bigger sprint review.

For instance, for a software development team, members may choose to conduct a short review in milestones with their product owner after each iteration is complete. After the review, the team may then discharge the new functionality to the website immediately.

Alternatively, the team may at the end of the entire work choose to have a review of the project in which case, they carry out all sprint review once at a time at the end of the entire iteration. Whichever method the team applies, it stills involves in Scrum.

What is GASP or NCSR?

Generally Accepted Scrum Practices (GASP) or Non-Core Scrum Rules (NCSR) are a set of activity carried out by a large number, and not necessarily all Scrum teams. Meanwhile, a team is not performing any activity would still be considered to be executing Scrum.

Teams' activities in the form of short, time-boxed iterations rather than a calendar month are not considered as GASP. Rather, it is a Scrum rule because, usually, Scrum encourages time-boxing rather than hourly estimation.

So, for any activity to pass as a GASP, it must be something that is generally accepted as a good idea. That goes to define a generally Accepted practice to mean that "every Scrum team should be aware of not involved in the practice.

Meanwhile, their non-involvement does not mean they are not excluded. Instead, they could elect to engage in some other practices outside what other Scrum teams do.

CHAPTER 7

USER STORIES AND CADENCE

A user story refers to a concise, brief descriptions of a feature. It is often told by and from the perspective of the user or customer of the system. It also means a short statement of a product requirement or a customer business case told by a product owner.

A user story can be written either by the end user or the team including the product owner, development team of Scrum Master. It should be expressed in plain language to help reader understand the power of the software.

The person who desires the new capability often writes a form of review of feedback as to how a system works. End users are often encouraged to discuss systems that they use rather than stating their features. User stories are often written on index cards or sticky notes and are saved in shoe box. They are also organized on walls or tables in order to facilitate discussion plans.

Telling a user story often follows a pattern like:

> "As a user (you can mention the category of user you fall into)/ I want/can (state the goal of your desired product)/so that (give reasons for waning the product)."

Example of User Stories:

- As a driver, I want to be able to accept credit card payment so riders can pay seamlessly.

- As a rider, I want to add my Master Card to my profile so I can pay without cash and

- As a driver, I want to be able to upload my profile photo and that of my vehicle so that I can attract more riders.

- As a rider, I want to be able to view as many as possible vehicles so that I can chose from a pool one that is suitable for me.

Who writes user stories?

This is one important question that has one single straight forward answer: anyone can write user stories. The first step is that the product Owner makes sure that that he creates a Product Backlog of Agile User Stories.

However, writing the User Story proper requires all hand to be on deck. It has been assumed in some quarters that the end user is always the one who writes a User Story. This is a wrong assumption. Any member of the team including the Product Owner, Team, Scrum Master, or external members like the end users of the stakeholders can write them.

Each team member in any Agile project as a matter of necessity is expected to have user story examples written by them. The

Figure 1: Examples of User Stories for Websites

conversation that generates stories is more important that who writes the story.

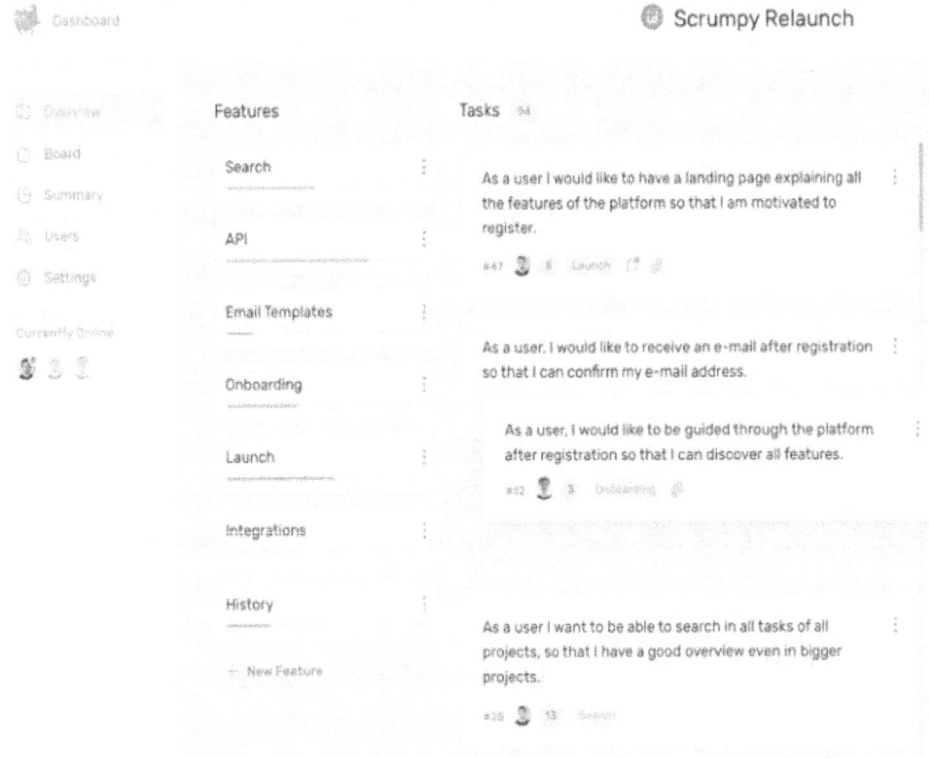

Tips to write excellent User Stories

You don't just write or tell a User Story. Consider it as an important aspect of your team project. In addition to the fact that you need to format the user story in such a way that it is always written from the customer's point of view, you need to take some important guidelines that will help you create a perfect User

Story. This will save you a lot of time discussing what exactly has to be built.

Here are a few trusted guidelines when generating a User Story:

1. Tell a story from Users Side

As the name suggests, a user story gives a description on how a product impacts on a customer. Either told by the user or the team, a user story must be written from the perspective of the software user or consumer. In another way, a user story describes how a customer uses or employs a product. Either way, the product must make impact on the bottom line of the user, and the story must be told from their perspective. Additionally, too, user stories must be targeted to capture a specific functionality of a product.

2. Tell a story; don't give a task

A story is not the same as a task. So, when telling or writing a user story, it must express feelings and give feedback. However, a user story requires several tasks to be able to deliver desired result and make needed impact. Here is the thing: task is concerned about implementation; user story is about definition. User stories must tell the 'what' about a product, not 'the how.'

3. Be simple, but stay high-level

Staying 'high-level' dos not suggest that your user story be isolated from your audience. No. You need to be accurate and straight to the point. The user stories must be written in plan, simple and solid language.

Doing this would help the team and stakeholders appreciate the needs and expectation of the user. Hence, it will help them avoid unnecessarily spending time explaining difficult terminology, buzzwords, and abbreviations.

4. Understand the users

It is important to stay up to date with trends and consumer needs. This will help you find out and study who the real users of your product are. From there, you can capture their expectations, get their profiles and points of view, and discover the associated 'pain points' using the software. Researching on user needs and other techniques could help generate insight into a better understanding of the key and real users.

5. Use epic stories

When writing user stories, one thing that is important is the use of epics. Epic user stories make a lot of deep impression on the reader. There are a number of ways you can use epics to convey your stories. One way is to take from across various different sprints, large amount of work to describe large pieces of functionality

Alternatively, since epics are for organizing stores and providing a bigger picture of impact, epics can come as grouping related smaller stories together to serve a common goal.

6. Prioritize stories, don't discard them

One thing to do to have great user stories and user story impact is to keep enriching your product backlog with new user stories.

Keep at describing new interaction scenarios with user, get at random ideas and include out of product impact activities.

Effective prioritization process also involves a proper grouping of new entries. As great practice, it helps to manage the potential noise. So, do not filter out or discard items from your backlog.

7. Prepare for success not just acceptance

One area many scrum teams don't consider is how a user story should affect acceptance of product. Beyond the 'it works' or 'oh, software X is a great product' feedback, you often get from users, your user story should help generate metrics which show direct user feedback and capture how your product makes users happy and engaged. Yes, acceptance helps you gain a good control of the development life-cycle of the feature; success makes a mid and long-term impact and value on the real users of your product.

8. #Tag stories

Depending on the complexity of your product, you need to use as many as hundreds of user stories. And if you use multiple user stories, it becomes easier for people to navigate and get along with hem if only you use hashtags.

Doing this will require you to name, organize, categorize and tag your stories. One mistake you should avoid is to rename or change a story description after the initial few revisions of a story.

You'll be bringing confusion to the audience and gaps in the team because of the inconsistency it will create.

Properly manage the metadata of your stories—status, progress, links, priorities, resources etc. This will help you explore, monitor, and understand your backlog.

Processes of a User Story

Typically, a User Story must go through three different important stages before it can be considered accepted. None of the three steps must not be missing in any User story you write. These features are Card, Confirmation and Conversation.

Card

The Card, otherwise called written text of the User Story, is a form of invitation and an upfront notification for conversation. One understanding about scrum is that the team does not necessarily have to write out all the items in the Product Backlog perfectly all at once. Changes and modification would occur along the line. Hence, the Card is an acknowledgement that both the customer and the team will continue to discover new areas of business needs as they are working on it.

>As a <user role> of the product,
>
>I can <action>
>
>So that <benefit>.

Conversation

The conversation refers to the collaborative discussion which is always facilitated at the expense and call of the Product Owner. The conversation involves all stakeholders and the team. The conversation can either be verbal or documented.

The conversation covers a wide range of issues. But most importantly, it is the hub of the real value of the user story. Issues raised during the conversation generate some of the things to be included in the user story. Hence, at every point in time, the Card should be modified to reflect the outcome and shared view of stakeholders and the team of this conversation.

Confirmation

The role of the Product Owner becomes more important here. No user story is consider done unless it has been confirmed by the product Owner. The team and the Product Owner check whether a story is complete or suitable for the purpose which it is set to achieve.

This assessment and eventual confirmation should be done in line with the Team's current definition of "done." Meanwhile, in the event that existing acceptance criteria do not consider the current definition of "done" in the eyes of the Team and Product Owner, new criteria should be established and inculcated to meet individual stories.

However, existing criteria must be well understood and agreed to by the Team before they are approved.

The INVEST criterion of User Story

Summarily, every User Story should fulfill the INVEST criteria proposed by Bill Wake, INVEST. INVEST stands for Independent, negotiable, Valuable, Estimable, Small, and Testable, and each is explained below:

Independent –User Stories are actually the smallest piece of work that can be told in any sequence. It means a change to one User Story doesn't affect the others. Each User Story is a unique self-sustaining piece of work.

Negotiable – There is no rigid or fixed workflow on how to execute User Stories. It is up to the team to unanimously agree how to carry them out.

Valuable – Each User Story represents some value to an end user and so must deliver a detached unit of it to them.

Estimable –The team can seamlessly guess the amount of time it will take to complete the development of a User Story.

Small – Each User Story must as small as they are must go through the whole sprint cycle of designing, coding, and testing.

Testable –The Team should establish a set of criteria that for acceptance to confirm whether or not a User Story is implemented appropriately and accepted widely by user.

How to split Agile User Stories

Interestingly, you don't have to be creating new stories all the time. Sometimes, you may need to spill a user story into the next line, especially if a user story is too large to fit into a Sprint. The best and simplest approach is to split it so it looks like an implied conjunction. Use words such as "and" or "or" in the text of the story to create two or more new stories from the parts.

There are various ways you can split a story, and these include: splitting by:

- Process step, that is, taking each step as a new story
- I/O channel – making each I/O channel a separate story
- User options – making the options become user stories
- Data range – that is, every range, whether by year, month or digit, becomes a new user story.
- CRUD action – create, read, update and delete. This is applicable only if action is related to business logic.
- Role/persona: each role becomes a separate story.

Cadence

Cadence in Agile is defined as the number of days or weeks that is contained in a single sprint or release. Put differently, cadence refers to the length of the team's development cycle. In recent, the length of time to make a complete sprint cycle has changed from organization to organization. The business environment has become pluralized that companies can decide how many days make a cadence.

Ideally, most organizations use a two-week sprint cadence. The cadence that a project or organization selects is always informed by a number of factors including risk, project type, and how vital, decisive ad crucial the project is.

The table below shows an example of cadence:

September 2019						
Sunday	Monday	Tuesday	Wednesday	Thursday	Friday	Saturday
			1	2	3	4
5	6	7	8	9	10	11
12	13	14	15	16	17	18

CHAPTER 8

SCRUM FLOW

The science of the scrum project implies that it follows a procedure. The whole systemic flow begins with a project vision. The vision defines every other thing that is to be developed. Certainly, the vision may look overcast from the start but as events unfold, it begins to take shape and becomes clearer.

The vision can be redefined over and over again, from market-based terms to system-based terms. The flow also consists in role assignment, with the Product Owner shouldering the responsibility of setting and delivering the vision to the project stakeholders and financiers with a view to maximizing their return on investment (ROI).

Furthermore, the Product Owner makes sure that he formulates a strategic plan for following up on prioritized project in the Product Backlog. Since the Product Backlog consists of a list of functional and nonfunctional requirements that deliver the project vision.

In the scum flow, the starting point is the organization of the Product Backlog. The Product Backlog is organized in such a way that items that will add value are given top priority with clear proposed releases. Organizing the Product Backlog consists of contents listing, prioritizing value-added items, and organizing of the Product Backlog, and then the proposed releases.

The Product Owner can effect changes to Product Backlog based on business requirements. The changes also depend on the speed level of the Team's ability to transform the Product Backlog to functionality.

All works on the scrum flow is done in sprint. Sprints refer to an iteration consisting of 30 repeated calendar days. Sprint consists of Sprint Planning, Sprint Review, Daily Scrum and Sprint Retrospective (See chapter 12 to read about the Scrum ceremonies).

There is a mutual collaboration between the Product Owner and the Development Team in the area of selecting priority items from the Product Backlog. While the Product Owner informs the Team what items in the Product Backlog he desires to be done; the Team in turn clarifies to the Product Owner how much of Product Backlog item desired list can be achieved and turn into functionality.

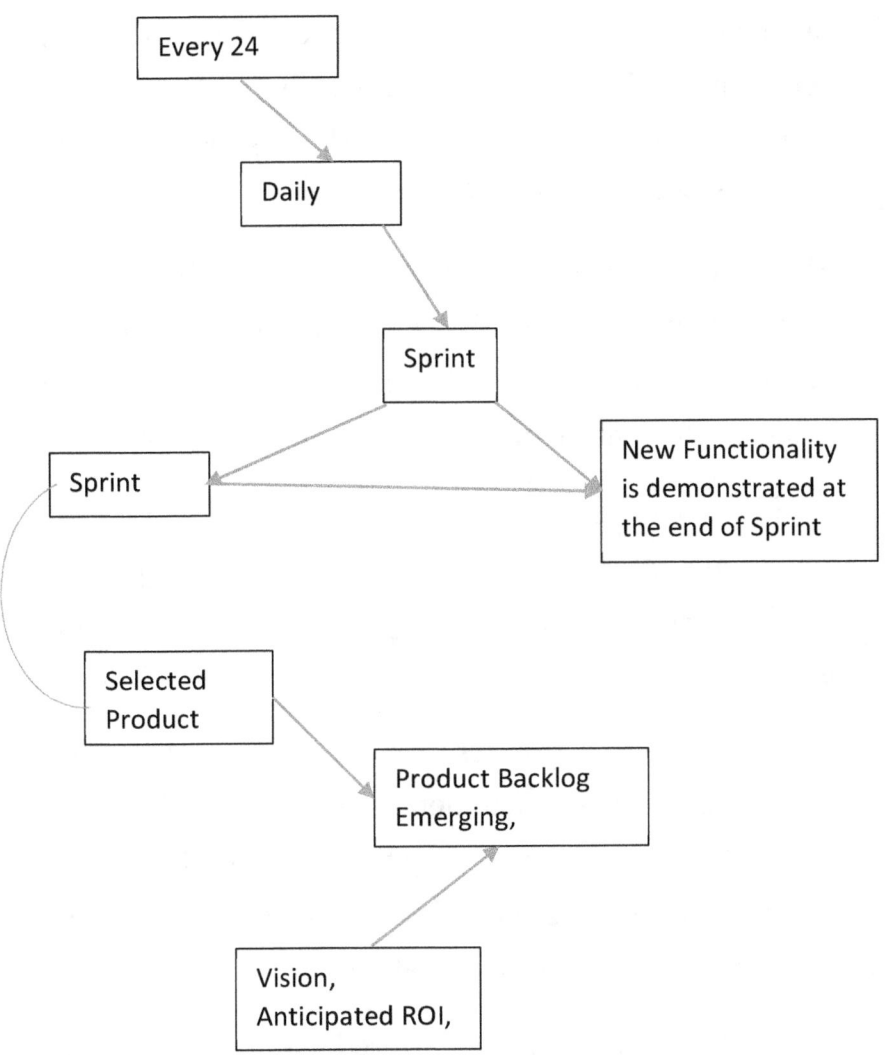

Scrum Process Flow

In our previous chapter discussion, we highlighted Scrum ceremonies, that is, the different activities and event that a scrum team undertakes before the completion of a sprint. How do these ceremonies relate and interact? Which one starts and which one ends the process? Now, we shall be having discussions around the flow of events during a sprint.

Simply put, Scrum process flow refers to the way to execute Scrum in the most effective, efficient way possible. It means the step-by-step procedure whereby teams can use the scrum to achieve efficient, high-quality results that optimize risk and maximize product delivery.

The scrum process flow starts with creating a product backlog up until we reach the backlog refinement stage, which entails review and revision of items in order to add detail, estimates and order.

During the scrum process, too, the product development team carries out the refinement details while the product owner update the backlog refinement at any time. During the sprint planning, the point where the team determines the sprint goal, the plan usually answers questions relating to

- What items can be delivered within the sprint increment?

- How will the work completed within this sprint achieve the increment goal?

- How will the chosen work get done?

It is at this stage to that the development team decides what task is to be completed within a sprint and how it should work, informing the product owner and Scrum master the product backlog priority items.

There is the daily Scrum, a meeting conducted by the development team and intended to enhance communication, remove endless meetings, identify bottlenecks that could lead to project impediments, and then promote quick decision-making.

The daily scrum allows the team to follow up on activities completed since the previous meeting. It also provides platform for team to prioritize work in the product backlog. The relevant questions to be answered at the daily Scrum meeting include:

- What did I do yesterday to help the team meet our goal?
- What will I do today to help the team meet our goal?
- Are there any bottlenecks or roadblocks that prevent me (or the team) from meeting the goal?

Scrum tasks

Scrum tasks are the subtle bits of work that are required to be done to give a finish to a story. Usually, a scrum task might taking the scrum team four to five hours to complete

On scrum task, team members can undertake to carry out tasks according to their skills and expertise. The sprint indicates the time remaining on a task and, on a daily basis, members who have offered can track the hours left to complete the task on the sprint.

However, if members undertaking the task are unable to meet deadline, then the remaining task is riven into additional tasks. Meanwhile, until the tasks is complete, a story is not added. It is (complete) task that informs the addition of story.

How to create and add Task

Usually, a task is added to an existing story using the Story form. There are specific locations on the Form where scrum tasks can be added. They are, the Tasks related list and the Add Scrum Tasks related link. However, scrum task can also be added using the planning board and the story progress board.

Creating Scrum Task

To create a scrum task using the Add scrum Task location on the Story Form, follow the following steps:

1. Navigate to Agile
2. Then> Stories > Open Stories
3. Open the desired story.
4. Click the Add Scrum Tasks related link.
5. Set the number of tasks to be created or added in the dialog box that appears:
    - Analysis
    - Coding

- Documentation
- Testing

6. Click OK to create a batch of tasks of the selected types in the Scrum Tasks related list.

   Scrum tasks created with this method are not yet complete and must be updated to become functional.

Open each scrum task record with a short description of ToDo and define the task.

7. Complete the form as described in the field description table.
8. Click Update to save your changes.

Eight Steps to a complete Scrum Process Flow

1. Determine the Product Backlog by listing product items and requirements in order of priority. This stage is carried out by the Product Owner in conjunction with Scrum Development Team.
2. Make estimate and plan for the workload based on the product Backlog items during the Product Backlog Refinement Meeting. This is carried out by Scrum team Development.
3. Hold a Sprint Planning, a meeting intended to define the sprint goal of the current iteration. Iteration is a duration of a Sprint, typically from 1 to 4 weeks. Select a list of User

Stories to form the Sprint Backlog for the next sprint which could help to achieve the sprint goal.
4. Complete the Sprint Backlog, giving each member of the Scrum team unit tasks based on the Sprint Backlog.
5. Conduct a Daily Scrum, which is a meeting required to discuss progress and make review. Each of the Daily Scrum is time-boxed, usually within 15 minutes. Every member of the team must speak face-to-face to discuss and interact with other members. The Daily Scrum always focus on past (what the team did and achieved yesterday), present (what it wants to do and accomplish today) and roadblocks (what could impede achieving Sprint goal), and update (reviewing team Sprint burn down chart).***[1]
6. Organize for each day a daily scrum that can be integrated and successfully compiled and showcased. Only release the version if the team endorses all of them and the unit test code is executed immediately.
7. The completion of user stories means the completion of the Sprint Backlog, and that signifies the end of a Sprint. After the completion of a Sprint, there is need to conduct a Sprint Review Meeting in which Product Owner and the customer must participate.

8. Finally, the Sprint Retrospective will be held after the sprint review at the end of each sprint. During the Sprint Retrospective, the team identifies by itself elements of the process that did or did not work during the sprint, along with potential solutions.

CHAPTER 9

SCRUM BURN DOWN AND VELOCITY

The Scrum Burn down Chart refers to a visual estimation tool which indicates the work done and completed in a day against the projected rate of completion for the current project release. The purpose of the scrum burn down chart is enable the team to track the progress of project ad deliver the expected result within the desired and stipulated schedule.

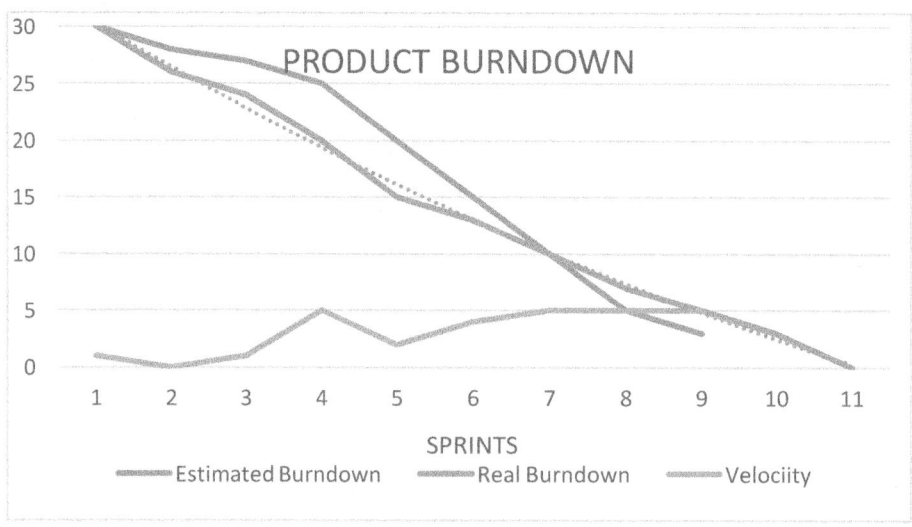

Figure 2: A sample of Burndown Chart

There are ways to execute the Burndown chart. It is important to know that stories in the Scrum should be burned down only in points and these have to be small. Secondly, planning poker must be used to estimate tasks in points and tasks must necessarily be burned down in points. Thirdly, the team must ensure that tasks burn down must be in hours.[2]

Velocity

The rate of progress of a Scrum development is called 'velocity.' It expresses the amount of story points or work a Scrum development can get completed per iteration or in a single sprint. In a more explicative form, velocity is an optional, but often used, indication of the average amount of Product Backlog that is turned into an Increment of product during a Sprint by a Scrum Team. Velocity is connected to the Scrum burn down because it is rate the Development Team within the Scrum Team works to achieve a project.

As events unfold, the entries in the Scrum Product Backlog will most likely change over time within the time allotted for the completion of the project. This would arise because new stories will be added; existing ones in the Product Backlog can be changed or deleted, depending on the Product Owner. Hence, in the simple Burndown Chart, the velocity of the Scrum Team and the change in the scope becomes indistinguishable (as we see in Figure 2 below).

---

[2] However, Scrum Foundation and ScrumIn no longer consider burning down tasks in hours as the best practice

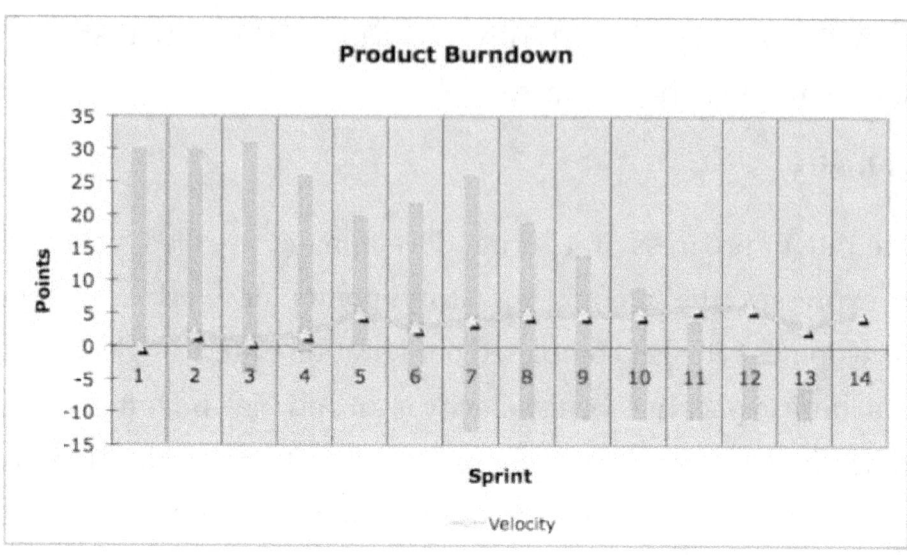

Velocity is a measure of the amount of work a Team can tackle during a single Sprint. Velocity is the key metric in Scrum. Velocity is always and should be tracked and calculated throughout the Sprint indicated on the Sprint Burn down Chart. The result of the calculated velocity should be visible to all members of the team. In that way, they will be able to measure whether or not changes they make are adding value to their productivity or not.

Ideally, Team velocity oscillate from one Sprint cycle to another and steadily trends upward by 10% on the Burn down chart in each Sprint. It takes the Team to complete three Sprints before it can determine its Velocity accurately. The Team and Product Owner must take their time to explain this to stakeholders, because the latter may not be ready to exercise patience until the three sprints elapse.

Purpose of the Velocity

Velocity serves a number of purposes including:

- It helps the team to get a feedback mechanism.
- With the velocity, the team can measure whether process changes they make are impacting positively or negatively on their productivity.
- Velocity also facilitates accurate forecasting by the team in terms of how many stories can be completed in a single Sprint. The Sprint forecasting is what is called *Yesterday's Weather* in Scrum.
- Velocity also helps in realizing Release planning.
- By knowing the Velocity, a Product Owner can be able to identify the number of Sprints it will take the Team to achieve a set level of functionality available for shipping.

How to calculate Velocity in a sprint

The velocity is calculated by counting only the user stories that are completed at the end of the iteration. It is forbidden to count the amount of work partially completed. An example of an incomplete work is to have a coding without testing.

Meanwhile, it is likely predictable to calculate the velocity of a Scrum Team and project the result after a conducting a few sprints. That is, Scrum Team has a latitude to give an estimated time left until all entries in the Scrum Product Backlog will be completed. However, it is not advisable to calculate points from a partially completed sprints. For stories. For instance, if the velocity of a Scrum Team is say, 30 story points and the total amount of work remaining is, say 155, it is easy for the team to put a figure of about 6 Sprint before it completes all stories in the Product Backlog.

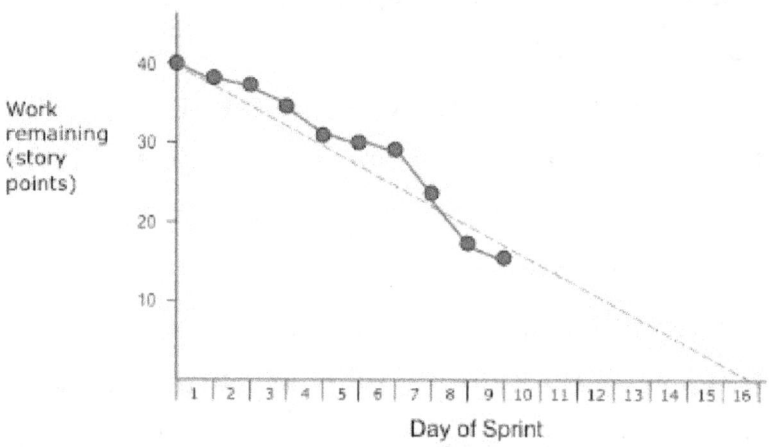

Question 1:

Calculate the velocity of the team in the following Burn down if, at the end of sprint, the team is only able to complete stories 1, 2 and 4.

Note: the team completed 50% of story 3, 40% of story 5.

Story 1 has 10 points

Story 2 has 4 points

Story 3 has 7 points

Story 4 has 3 points

Story 5 has 8 points

Solution 1:

The first rule in a burn down a partially completed story does not count. The team can only measure a potentially usable product increment. Hence, the velocity for that sprint would be 17.

However, if the team is able to complete the remaining 50% of the story 3 and 60% of story 5 in the next sprint, they would add 15 more points to make the velocity 32 points.

Question 2:

Calculate the velocity of a team in the following stories if the team is able to complete stories 1 and 2.

Story 1 has 5 points

Story 2 has 4 points

Solution 2:

The velocity for that sprint is 9.

Differences between the velocity chart and burn down chart

Sprint burn down chart

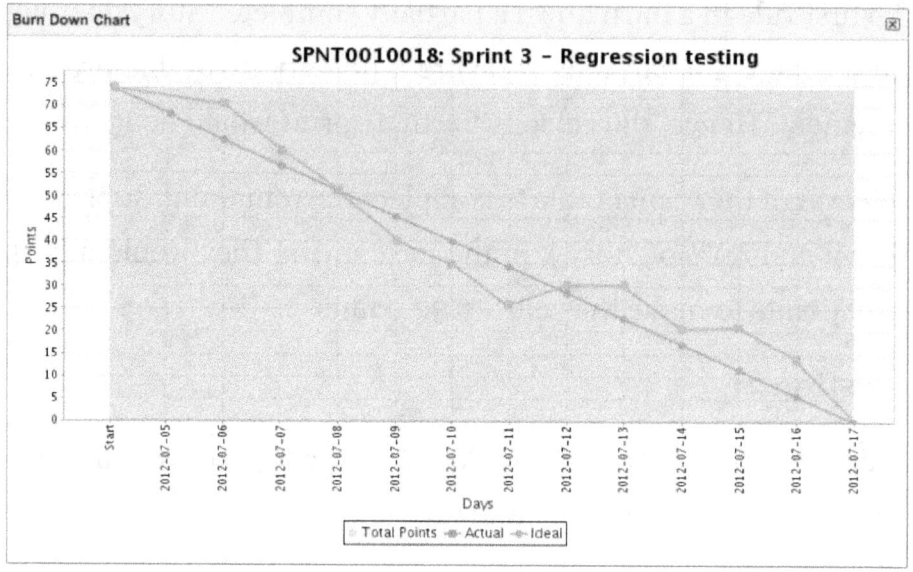

Figure 3b:

In the example in the chart above, the blue line indicates the ideal progress for the sprint from start to finish while the red line stands for the actual progress the scrum team made during the sprint.

Team progress just below the blue line is where team activity surpassed the ideal slope as team members completed more story points than desired. The upward slope shows the introduction of additional stories which means additional points. The team was able to complete 15 points of work in the final day of the sprint.

Burn down chart	Velocity chart
The burn down chart shows the virtual progress a release team is making on a project in a sprint from start to finish against the real time actual daily progress.	The velocity chart indicates the estimated effort calculated in story points that a release team is able to delivered across multiple sprints.
The purpose of the burn down chart is to help the scrum master to be able to manage the releases and sprints in a more efficient way in a day-to-day fashion	The chart provides the scrum master an insight into the general ability of the development team over time.
	The velocity chart helps determine how many points worth of work can be completed per sprint for a given team
It helps the scrum master to be able to track and address issues coming up.	It allows for more accurate sprint planning

The Burn down chart displays comparisons of outstanding work against available time.	A team velocity chart shows the effort (as points) for a specific team against multiple sprints and multiple releases.
	Velocity charts for releases display team performance across the sprints in a specific release.

Figure 2$_a$ represents Velocity chart while *Figure 2$_b$* represents Burn down chart

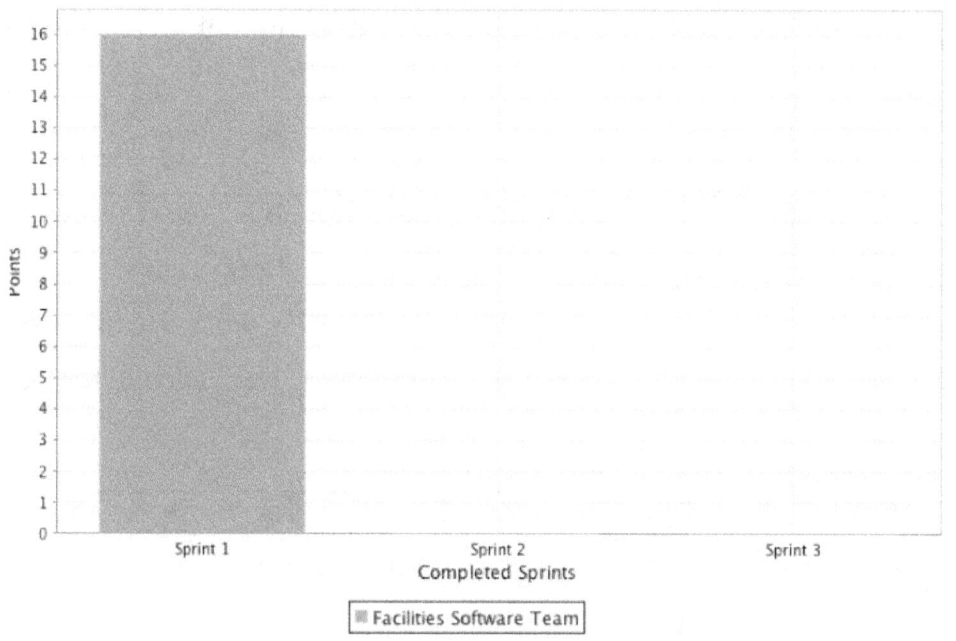

Figure 2a:

CHAPTER 10

SCRUM ARTIFACTS

This is one component part of the Scrum framework that you wouldn't want to miss. Let us go a bit archeological for a moment. The nomenclature may be the same, the role and meaning of artifacts in archeological studies do not also change as it applies to the Scrum framework. However, different system with different modes of application of terms.

What do artifacts mean in archeology? They refer to objects that are made by humans. Simply put, artifacts are products of human creativity. They are works of art, made either in the form of a tool to solve a problem or as an invention intended to inspire.

Similarly, the Scrum system is designed with some artifacts. Basically, there are three primary artifacts that the Scrum framework describes. They are:

- The Product Backlog
- The Sprint backlog
- The Product Increment

Other artifacts include Sprint Retrospectives and Product backlog Refinement. Each of these artifacts is for the umpteen time integral to the overall usage of the system.

The purpose of the artifacts in the Scrum is essentially to maximize transparency, and promote a share understanding of the work in a team. While the Sprint Backlog and Product Backlog are responsible for defining the work to be done that will enhance work value, the Product Increment refers to the achieved portion of the work done work during a particular duration or sprint.

The Product Backlog

The Product Backlog is the portion of the Scrum project that sets scale of reference. By that the segment answers the fundamental question relating to 'what is the most important task to build next? In simple terms, Product Backlog can be described as constantly evolving artifacts that are ongoing.

The segment serves as the roadmaps that set the tone for what is to be done at each stage of the project. It is important to note that the Product Backlog is open to modification, constant update and refinement in order to suit the changes that occur as a result of dynamic nature of product development.

Managing your product backlog

This is one thing many Scrum practitioners have to get familiar with. It is crucial to always make effort to keep your product backlog small and manageable. You're likely to face three key intractable issues if you keep stocking your product backlog with too many items. They include:

- **Consumes unnecessary time**

Working with too many items in the product backlog makes work delivery harder and in the process large amount of time is lost. This is because the time it takes to sort out the items packed up haphazardly in the backlog is always longer than the time it would take to arrange. Prioritization becomes harder and there is higher chances that items are duplicated.

- **Team Progress is hardly noticeable**

Due to time lost in packing up items in the product backlog, the Scrum Team hardly notices progress they make. For instance, a team that finishes 20 of 70 items are likely to see the progress they make. However, when a team completes 20 of 900 fee frustrated as the sense of accomplishment and drive to continue would obviously diminish.

- **Shortens human capital**

Imagine a five-member team having to carve out two members to concentrate sorting out items in the product backlog. That approach is unhealthy for speed, urgency, and achievement. If someone has to spend valuable time creating all those product backlog items, then it reduces the chance of achieving the visibility projected into the future from the start of the work.

In order to avoid facing the above snags, what must a team do? To be able to effectively manage your team's product backlog, keep it small and never have it item-clogged, the following steps will be useful.

Remove items you'll never realistically do

Once you find out that there are items in the product backlog that the team would not realistically be able to do, it is advisable to ruthlessly purge them as quickly as possible from the product backlog. In that way, you will be able to keep your product backlog small and manageable.

Although this may be hard to achieve, and sometimes come with some shock situations in which you need to make contingency, a leader should be highly proactive in thinking ahead of team members in generating on-the-spot ideas to rescue the situation.

Keep off 'not-at-the-moment' items

One other strategy akin to the above is keeping off the product backlog items that the team is not ready for now. Yes, the product owner wants those items, but is the team currently ready to work on them? How fairly soon would the items be needed? Is the owner ready for pay for them now?

If the answer to the first is no, then take them off the shelf. If it is yes to the third, then retain them and keep off other ones that are not needed right away. If the team is not disposed now to work on them and would not be ready for them in the nearest foreseeable future, kindly delete them off the product backlog.

Instead of clogging your product backlog, create a holding tank where you can keep standby items until they are ready to be treated by the team. Doing that would keep your product backlog small and manageable.

Product backlog needs periodic review

Consider the product backlog as your wardrobe where you keep the clothing. How often do you check? I guess daily. That is exactly how you should treat your product backlog. If not daily, as you do your wardrobe, at least make it a point of duty to periodically (maybe quarterly) review your product backlog.

Keeping your product backlog to a reasonable size is no brainer. Initiate a regular review process, to check the fancy and non-fancy items. In fact, the product owner can help in this regard, helping you to clean up, delete, or move items that the team won't work on or items that do not drive immediate attention of the team.

Product Backlog Refinement

Before we move to the next Scrum Artifact, it is important we discuss the product backlog refinement process. Our previous knowledge puts us in the understanding that Product Backlog refers to constantly evolving artifacts that are never complete.

If some artifacts are ongoing, something must be the chief initiator of such work. This is the role the Product Backlog Refinement plays. So, Product Backlog refinement refers to the activity executed to constantly evolve. It becomes clear that the Product Backlog Refinement occupies a central and constant place in the life of the Product Backlog, because it keeps evolving new product backlog.

Sprint Backlog

As Scrum artifacts, the Sprint Backlog refers to a list of tasks the Scrum team has identified and itemized to be completed during the Scrum sprint. Usually, during the sprint meeting when a Development team sets out its plan, the team often chooses some number of product backlog items, usually in the form of user stories. Hence, the team identifies the tasks necessary to give a finish touches to each user story.

Also, the spring backlog can be understood to contain two quick calls to action. One, think of it as the 'How' of the Sprint and the 'What' of the Sprint. By the 'What', we means task to be completed by the team. The 'How' stands for the way such tasks would be delivered.

The Sprint Backlog represents a highly evidently planned out, real-time picture of the work that the Development Team plans to accomplish during the Sprint. The sprint backlog is an item only excusive to the Development Team

Besides having the two important components of 'How' and 'What' of the Sprint, Sprint Backlog also consists of the Development Team's design for how the team would carry out and deliver the product Increment.

It all depends on you, you could maintain your sprint backlog using any of the available software products designed specifically for Scrum. The Scrum framework also allows you to represent your sprint backlog as a spreadsheet or deploy your defect tracking system. The table below is an example of how you can maintain your sprint backlog.

The following are the important contents of the Sprint backlog:

1. Tasks that have been decomposed from the user stories and accepted by the Team for the current iteration.
2. Story points or time estimations for individual tasks.
3. Product backlog Refinements of the "definition of work done" as it concerns a specific story or task.
4. Product Backlog Refinements to stories that don't compromise the Sprint Goal or require the Product Owner to call for an early closure of the Sprint.
5. In-sprint stories or tasks added by the Team to give teeth to the current Sprint Goal.

Again, it needs to be emphasized that the Team could at the Spring Planning stage sets out the Sprint Goal and stories accepted for the current Sprint. However, Team updates and modifies tasks and sometimes stories on the Sprint Backlog when they see the need to do so in other to support the Sprint Goal.

Ideally, updating the sprint backlog per day is ok. However, as soon as new information is available during sprint, members of team can update the sprint backlog. Other teams could choose to do their update during the daily scrum. Usually, the estimated work left undone on the schedule is calculated and put into graphical representation using the ScrumMaster, and it will look like the chart below:

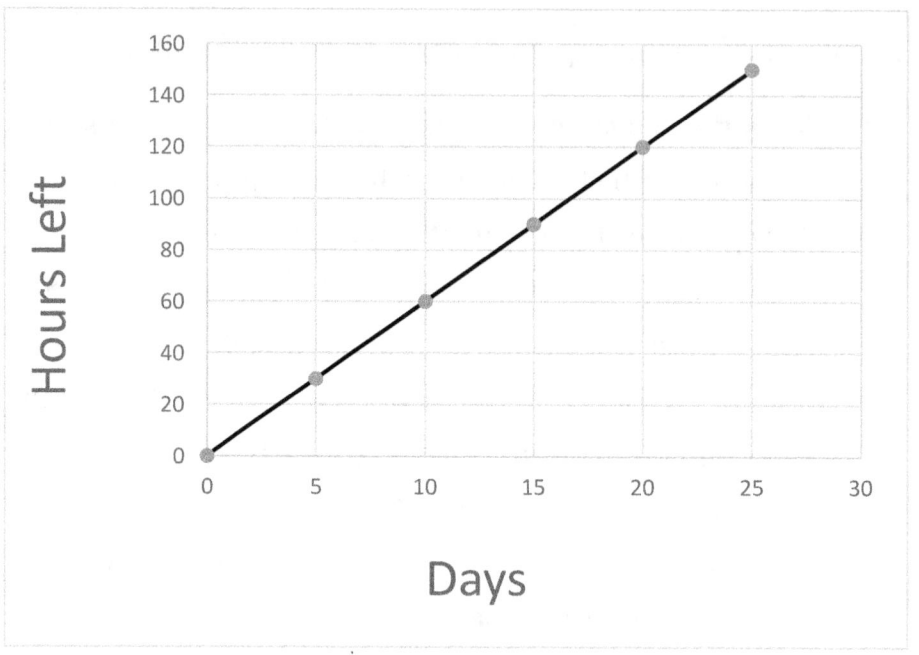

In the sprint backlog graph shown in chapter 1, what we observe is that the team in this scenario jerked in too much work at the initial stage into the sprint backlog. Yet, they had about sufficient hours to go on day 5 of a 25-day sprint.

Meanwhile, product owner had to add some user stories from the sprint, resulting in the big he rise on the chart from day 1 to 25. The graph makes consistent progress, finishing the Scrum sprint successfully

It is very crucial that the team pulls the accurate amount of work done, completed and remaining into the Scrum sprint. The team can also add or remove tasks.

Scrum Focus Areas

What do you have to focus on in Scrum framework?

- **Focus on Team Performance**

It is worth re-emphasizing that it is in team success you that find the skills and commitment of each member. After all, nobody commends perfect rehearsals; people applaud excellent output.

So, with Scrum, you're not looking for a strategy that sets to distinguish individual members of a team. Rather it seeks to identify and then harness the potentials, expertise, skills and experience that reside in individual members of your team. In doing that, Scrum focuses on team performance, measuring corporate and not individual performance.

- **Relative Task Comparison**

How do you measure performance of team tasks in your company? Estimating member's effort based on number of hours? That absolutely is not going to produce desired and desirable results. Scrum comes with an incredible different approach that works.

The system operates on the principle of relative estimation of task based on complexity and size. In other words, relative estimation preferably works better as a method of sizing up member's effort. The idea is that when you compare in relative terms individuals' tasks based on their complexity and size, rather than number of hours spent, the result you're going to get would be less prone to error.

- **Engage Time Boxing**

This is one novel approach project managers and expert company progress analysts find highly useful. Scrum focuses on gaining commitment and speed by time boxing. By that, the strategy evolves the practice of allocating task to a specific iteration.

Through this, each iteration has an equal, fixed duration within which each task is to be completed. This is in contrast to existing model—especially the Kanban, which achieves commitment and speed by limiting work in progress.

- **Evaluate Team Happiness Indicators**

This is a key feature in Scrum. Measuring happiness indicators of your team at the end of a project is a concept motivated by the idea that team performs better in future tasks once they express happiness and satisfaction with the outcome of the project at hand.

As a manager, therefore, it is important to tract, appreciate, measure, and evaluate the leading motivating factors that enhance the interest and happiness of the rest of the team.

- **Focus on goal not roadmap**

Scrum framework does not discourage the use of roadmap while setting out on a project. However, roadmap should rather serve as a guide and not a cast in stone kind of thing. With Scrum system, every sprint has its own uniqueness, and the roadmap can be modified to suit the goal of each sprint.

Put simply, roadmaps are loose visions at best. Historical performance and lessons have a crucial role to play to dictate or inform changes that would occur from sprint to sprint. This leads to what is called 'velocity' in Scrum system. By velocity, teams are believed to decide and define their capacity by looking at their performance in the past.

- **Adopt Commitment to Process Improvement Approach**

Commitment to continuous improvement of processes is a core aspect of Scrum. Jeff Sutherland's invention works with the goal that every stage of iteration ideally should produce enhanced results that improve on the outcome of last performance. Process improvement in Scrum is a strategy that focuses on milestone improvements, technically called *kaizen*.

CHAPTER 11

SCRUM CEREMONIES

Scrum Ceremonies

Scrum ceremonies remain one of the vital force and components of the Agile software delivery process. They refer to the gathering and coming together of Scrum team with a view to getting work done in an organized, structured manner.

As the name suggests, Scrum ceremonies are meetings not just for the sake of it of fun. Rather, scrum ceremonies offer the platform for scrum team to effectively empower, influence, brainstorm, collaborate, and help each other to grow and ultimately drive results.

If scrum ceremonies are not properly managed they can become mere jamborees where the team spend a lot of invaluable time gallivanting and overwhelmingly waste productive time of their calendars and whittle down the purpose and value of their coming together.

Another end for which the Scrum ceremonies are often organized is to realize and enable many of the Agile core values and principles, some of which include work progress review, customer satisfaction, sustainable effort, team work, effective communication, among others.

While it is important for team to hold these ceremonies regularly, sometimes, they may abandon them, either because the team does not see the need and value for them at the time or they have jettisoned the core values and principles. In either way, it is dangerous for team to not hold scrum ceremonies.

What are the Scrum Ceremonies?

Now, let us discharge the four scrum ceremonies and the purpose for which they are important to the overall scrum and agile drive. The key facilitating factors for effective scrum ceremonies include purpose, attendees, tips and tricks.

The best way to start this section is to proclaim unequivocally that Scrum is deliberately a simple and lightweight process. However, its mastering can become or be made difficult, especially if its cores goals of serving as a framework for cross-functional teams to unravel complex issues are not taken seriously.

Scrum ceremonies provide the platform where these complex problems can be discussed and resolved. They help expand the scope and bring niceties to unstructured framework.

It is important to bear in mind that these ceremonies are tied to specific activities and goals of the scrum framework. In simple terms, we could consider scrum ceremonies as a great Agile process that team deploys globally to develop strategy that is actionable. The scrum ceremonies include:

1. Sprint Planning
2. Daily Scrum
3. Sprint Review
4. Sprint Retrospective

1. **Sprint Planning**

Sprint Planning

Just as the name indicates, sprint planning consists of the set of arrangement, scheduling and design organized to make sure the development team is adequately and properly prepared to achieve a goal and get work done every sprint.

When the team meets at the beginning of a new sprint, the purpose is often to design for Product Owner and Development team to do a review of the prioritized product Backlog. One thing that is important to note here is that the prioritized product Backlog should contain only items that the team would be able to complete at the end of the sprint.

Sprint Planning as a Scrum ceremony, is essentially organized for the purpose of engaging in a series of productive discussions, negotiations, and brainstorming that ultimately target generating a sprint backlog that contains only all items the team is committed to achieving during the course of one single sprint cycle.

These achievable items could be tagged the sprint goal, a demonstrable increment of work that can be proven at the end of a sprint. The items should be agreed upon by all team members, in that way, they are able to work together towards achieving them.

Who should attend Sprint Planning Ceremony?

In simple answer, all scrum roles should be in attendance. Each one has an eminently important role in Sprint Planning facilitation in order to ensure a successful deliberation. As a matter of fact, every Sprint Planning has in attendance the Product Owner, Scrum Master and Development Team.

What does the Product Owner do during Sprint Planning?

Apart from the Scrum Master, the Product Owner shoulder a lot of pre-meeting responsibility, preparing the entire roles for the Sprint Planning. For instance, the Product Owner has the responsibility to prepare the Product Backlog and ready for review ahead of the meeting.

In addition, the Product Owner should add acceptance criteria, requirements and all other necessary details for the Development Team that would give a detailed and accurate estimate of the level of effort and performance.

All grey areas in terms of possible questions and assumptions that the Development team may have the product Owner should anticipate and clarify. In that way, they have a blueprint of what the team is going to do and achieve in a sprint.

What about Scrum Master?

Scrum Master is primarily responsible for facilitating the entire session of the Sprint Planning. They play the active role of ideal facilitator, making sure all questions and assumption of the Development Team which answer have been prepared by the Product Owner are adequately addressed. The timing, duration, Q &A session, and closing of the meeting are responsibilities due the Scrum Master.

And the Development Team?

The Development Team is not a spectator or onlooker during Sprint Planning. They form an integral part of the whole session. They must be reasonably critical of the outline and responses of the Product Owner. The prepare questions about items to be pulled into the Product Backlog for the entire sprint.

What is the length of Sprint Planning?

The length of a Sprint Planning ceremony depends largely on the length of the sprint. So, if the duration of your sprint is two weeks, then your Sprint Planning should not last more than 3 to 4 hours, max; for a week-long sprint, the Sprint Planning should last not more than 2 hours.

2. Daily Scrum

Alternatively named the daily standup, daily scrum refers to a quick pulse check that not only defines the work for the day for the team but more importantly illuminates the team to identify all roadblocks to team progress.

Also called a scrum meeting, this meeting offers the team opportunity to come together and define what the day's work outline should look like, identifying any impediments and prospect.

What's need for Daily Scrum?

The goal of the daily Scrum is primarily to do a review and progress overview of their daily activity. It is a platform that provides the team with a frequent chance to communicate individual and corporate progress. A

All of the talking and deliberation should be geared towards achieving that common goal set out at the beginning of the sprint. Daily Scrum helps the team to identify work blockers and proffer solution on how to remove them.

Who does what during Daily Scrum?

The Scrum Master has the responsibility of shouldering the clearing of bottlenecks to the achievement of goals by the

Development Team. This would help the Development team achieve more and focus on delivering the work identified in Sprint Planning.

The Development team executes all planned work and activity. Although they take active part in the entire Sprint planning and Daily Scrum asking questions, giving possible roadmap, the Development Team caries out all activities post-daily scrum.

During each daily scrum, the Development Team gives answers to the following important questions:

- What did you do yesterday?
- What will you do today?
- Are there any impediments in the way?

Although the presence of the Product Owner is optional during daily scrum, he is strategic in preparing the entire roles ahead of the daily standup. They prepare answers to any blockers or roadblocks that the team may identify.

How long should a daily scrum take?

Ideally, since a daily scrum is to review, outline day's work and identify impediments, it should not last more than 15 to 20 minutes. However, it can stretch more than that depending on workload in the previous day. But, a daily scrum should be kept short and simple to allow the Development Team and other stakeholders get on to work early.

3. **Sprint Review**

In simple terms, sprint review means 'stakeholder, kindly have an assessment of our completed work.' That sounds too simplistic, right? That is exactly what it is. During Sprint Review ceremonies, all finished work are displayed by the Development Team to the stakeholders. However, the Scrum Master and Product Owner are not excluded in the session.

They come together to showcase the outcome of the work they have done during a sprint cycle to stakeholders to have their own assessment.

Why Sprint Review?

Just like you have to show your teachers at the end of the term how much study your have assimilated by going to write exam, so also at the end of each sprint, you have to be assessed.

Again, just to remind you of the routine in your old school days: as you're about rounding off an academic term, there used to be a window of opportunity where you have review of all that transpired. The same rule and procedure apply here.

The platform also provides opportunity for stakeholders to take a look at what has been done and have a sooner than later feel of possibly what to expect. The stakeholders can quickly adapt the product that form the result of the effort of the Development team.

It is important to keep in mind that work showcased during Sprint Review should be shippable to the extent that they meet the definition and scope of what was defined at the begging of the sprint. This would boost the stakeholders' confidence in the team and particularly the Development Team gets much of the thumb-up.

Again, Sprint Review is not time for the team to panic or shiver like an average PhD student preparing for his Thesis defense. No. Sprint Review, which is alternatively called Sprint Demo, is an interactive session where Development Team displays what they have been able to achieve over the course of a sprint cycle to stakeholders.

It is geared towards building trust and confidence the stakeholders repose in the team and thus strengthens the relationship between the two parties. It serves as the face-to-face manner for stakeholders to have an early feedback from customers and objective assessment of what has been done by the team.

Again, it should be done in a relaxed mood as it is intended to show the business value the completed work would bring to the product development. The team should ensure they do everything possible to impress the outsider reviewers and external evaluators

When is Sprint Review Appropriate?

The team can decide to have the Sprint Reviews staged on a causal "Demo Friday" or make it a kind of organized event where everyone is seated, looking serious!

Who is needed in attendance?

Everyone! Anyone! From the Product Owner to Scrum Master, to Development, attendance is crucial. This is the time the entire team is showing they are up to the task they are charged with. Their delivery would inform stakeholders how competent or otherwise the entire team is. Also in attendance are a blend of management, internal and external stakeholders, end users, and developers from other projects.

It is the responsibility of the Scrum Master and Product Owner to be engage in discussions on who should be in attendance during the Sprint Review. Interestingly, the Sprint Review is more open to attendees than other Scrum ceremonies. It is a fluid event that offers opportunity for insider and outsider assessment of the team.

How long should it take?

If you think of the duration for the Sprint Planning, then you get a sense of how long the sprint review should take. Preferably, an hour a week of the sprint should be enough. If for, instance, you have a two-week sprint, a two-hour Sprint Review should be scheduled.

4. Sprint Retrospective

If you're looking for a platform to get technical during Scrum ceremonies, then Sprint Retrospective is not the right place for you. Maybe, you can check Scrum Planning. However, Sprint Retrospective represents the final lap in the series of scrum ceremonies in which the team can look back do a thorough appraisal.

While other scrum events and ceremonies may offer you the not-too-serious, not-too-relaxed mood, Sprint Retrospective takes the anti-Aristotelian extreme virtue by giving us a too-serious platform. It is an opportunity for the team to ask questions about the feedback they get after showcasing the work they have completed. Here, the team looks back to see completed work and identify items that could be improved.

What's in for the Team?

Great question! After Sprint Review has been done and stakeholders and participants have given their respective review and feedback, the team needs to now sit down and see how they ca improve on subsequent deliveries.

It is during Sprint Retrospective that the scrum team can discuss situations that are going on fine; access the ones that need improvement and suggest possible ways to enhance work delivery. The fundamental questions that the team often confront itself with during the Sprint Retrospective include:

- What went well over the last sprint?
- What didn't go so well?
- What could we do differently to improve?

Sprint Retrospective Should Drive Change Not Blame

Sprint Retrospective should be an avenue not for blame game or castigating a team member for doing or not doing something; rather, the session should be a blameless space for members to give their honest and objective feedback and recommendations.

Simply put, it should be a forward-projecting rather than a backward-looking space. Essentially it should drive desirable and desired change for the team. For this to happen, all recommendation, data and feedback got from members and participants should be collated and gradually implemented where appropriate to further strengthen the team's future performance.

Who should Retrospect?

At every Sprint Retrospective meeting, the Scrum Master and the Development Team. Should be in attendance. Meanwhile, participation of Product Owner is an optional thing. Outside stakeholders can be in attendance too.

What about duration?

Being a session for feedback, Sprint Retrospective meetings should be longer than a Spring Review in terms of duration. However, it should not exceed the maximum period of 1 hours thirty minutes, for a two-week sprint. But if you are having one-month sprint, then your Sprint Retrospective can take as much as 3 hours.

Below is a chart representing the maximum allotted duration for each Scrum ceremony facilitation for a four-week Sprint:

Summary of Scrum Ceremonies

Agile is focused on constant and gradual improvement and driving change, hence all ceremonies should be driven towards ensuring better quality service delivery. The team should be motivated at every session of the events to have a progressive approach to the work.

While the team is expected to improved, resources to be used should also be enhanced; approach should also become more efficient and effective to achieve more with little. Needless to say that Scrum ceremonies should be forums where every member is shown the capacity and potentials that reside in them.

CHAPTER 12

THE SCRUM CORE AND NON-CORE ROLES

There is nothing weird or out-of-this-world about the term Scrum Roles. It refers to the daily use of role assignment in our offices. But here is the difference, scrum roles are focused on the team and not on individuals.

They reflect the collective roles individuals play in achieving collective result. In scrum, there are basic groups who perform certain roles towards project management and software development. They include the product owner, scrum master, and development team.

Let us discuss each of the Scrum core roles.

1. The Product Owner

Allegorically, there is no building without a builder; so also, no project is executed in a vacuum. As the name suggests, the product owner is the person who owns the product. Maybe, that sounds circular. In Scrum, a product owner represents the client and the business for the product on which they're working. The product owner possesses the backlog. They determine which items take precedence over others. They are responsible for setting the tune for every sprint or iteration by striving to give priority beforehand to items to be worked on.

The survey the market and the industry to identify needs and expectations of customers and then make informed executive product decisions on a daily basis. In the process, they ultimately help in translating those needs into actionable work items for the Development team.

2. The Scrum Master

As much as a team desires that work must be delivered quicker and to taste, workers must be adequately equipped with all the resources they need to achieve this goal. So, there are workers; there are those responsible for making things work.

A Scrum master belongs to the second group. He is that person responsible for ensuring the team has everything they need to deliver value. A scrum master could be a coach, facilitator, motivator, moderator, mediator, counselor, advocate, or a mediator.

The Scrum master must be one who is capable of projecting into the future, foreseeing challenges before they turn into project impediments. Hence, he is an impediment remover.

He facilitates the process of making sure there constant and smooth communication channels among members of the team. As an advocate, the Scrum master serves as the middle man between development team and the product owner.

He mediates to ensure that all facility needed are in place before they are needed. As a matter of fact, a Scrum master coordinates all activities; he is the project manager in scrum. So, whatever duties and responsibilities you think a project manager should do, the scrum master should.

3. The Development Team

Delivering working software is no joke. It requires not just a vision; it must be driven by a team. A development team refers to a group of cross-functional and multi-purpose team members who are focused on ensuring delivery of working software.

The Development Team, also called the Scrum Team, consists of all persons involved in the technical aspect of a project. They include professionals, software development newbies, experts, novices, designers, QA who collaborates collaborate on the actual development of a product.

Usually, the development team is composed of 5-10 people who are fully dedicated to working out a scrum project. However, reality may change the course of things in which case agencies might take a different approach based on the challenges they grapple with.

In any case, ideally, the development team adequately aided by the facilitation of the Scrum Master and Product Owner, should be a self-organizing and self-motivated group of individuals who offers value.

Non-core Roles

Non-core roles are those roles which are not mandatory or required for the scrum project to run effectively. These roles consist of members who only interested and willing to be part of the project from an outsider point of view. They are not directly involved in the day-to-day running and core implementation of the scrum project. Unlike the core roles, the non-core roles have no formal role they play in relation to the scrum project.

They may assist and interface with the project team but do not have any official responsibility towards the success of the project. However, they non-core roles as we have seen in our previous discussions serve as the third-eye that keeps the team on its toes to be able to achieve optimal result. Hence, the non-core roles should be taken into consideration when the team is making decision on the Scrum project.

Their continuity may be ceased by the team at any time, but it is not advisable that the team scraps members of the non-core roles on any project. As we see in the Sprint Review session, the stakeholders are very important in giving feedback and ensuring the team goes back and improve on the project they come to showcase.

The non-core role participants in the scrum project include:

1. **Stakeholders**

By stakeholders, we refer to a number of interests. It is a collective term that refers to the assortment of individuals who volunteer to be part of the project. Some stakeholders participate in the project only as consumers; others take part as sponsors. Basically, stakeholders in the Scrum project include customers, users, and sponsors.

These people constantly interface with the Product Owner, Scrum Master and Development Team. They duty though no formal is to provide the core role members with valuable inputs that would help in improving showcased projects. They also facilitate creation of the project's product, service, or other result.

Stakeholders are also important person who could influence the project throughout its developmental stages. They play active role in other stages including Develop Epic(s), Create Prioritized Product Backlog, Conduct Release Planning, and Retrospect Sprint.

2. Customer

Every product has an end user and consumer. Product or service without patronage is dead on arrival. So, when a scrum project is being designed by the Product owner, there must be a consumer in mind who will purchase and use them. In fact, consumer has been described as the life wire of company sustenance. We may ask: who is the scrum project consumer?

The consumer is the individual or a corporate body that subscribes to acquire the product or service of manufacturer or service provider. In relation to scrum, the consumers are those persons and organizations who desire to use Scrum product.

Scrum products' consumers can be either internal customers, that is those within the team or external customers, that is, those who have no formal link with the organization where Scrum is being applied.

3. Users

There is a little difference between a consumer and a user. A user refers to the individual or the organization that directly utilizes Scrum project's product, service, and other result. At some time, a user can be the consumer; at other times, they are not.

However, like consumer, users form part of the non-core role participants in any organization. Users can be those within the organization or those outside. But whether an internal user or external user, the role of the user cannot be overemphasized.

4. Sponsor

In a way the sponsor is a major stakeholder in any project. The sponsor refers to an individual or corporate organization that is putting down the funds to keep a project going. They provide the resources, whether human or infrastructure as well as technical and operational support for the project. As a stakeholder then, the sponsor is one to whom the organization is also accountable.

5. Scrum Guidance Body

The Scrum Guidance Body (SGB) is one of the non-core optional role in the scrum project. The SGB is a collection of brochures and a group of professionals and experts who characteristically participate in defining objectives related to quality, regulations, security, and other key organizational parameters.

The objectives defined by the Scrum Guidance Body help to guide the work done by the team, which includes the Product Owner, Scrum Master, and the Scrum Development Team. Also, the SBG also supports capture the best practices that should be used during the implementation of all Scrum projects in the organization.

However, the Scrum Guidance Body does not have power to make decisions in connection with the Scrum project. The SGB only can act as a consulting body which only guides the hierarchy levels in the project organization

The structure of the Scrum Guidance Body serves as the advisory body for the portfolio, program, and project of the project organization. The Scrum Team may or may seek advice from the Scum Guidance Body. The optional role of the SGB does not mean that they are unimportant.

6. Vendors

Vendors are non-core role players in the project organization. They are internal or external individuals or organizations that provide products and services that are not available within the core competencies of the project organization. It is possible that vendors can also act as the same person or organization, playing the role of a stakeholder, sponsor, or customer.

CHAPTER 13

SCALING SCRUM

Disclaimer!!!

Here is the first thing to say, a sort of disclaimer before you even conceive the idea of scaling Scrum: Will scaling resolve my issues. If not, don't. That sounds daunting, right? Not so as you may think. It is important that warning comes earlier so you don't regret what ordinarily you should have avoided.

Let's us put that behind us, but at the back of our mind now that we are about to explain the dynamics of scaling Scrum.

The essence of scaling is to resolve issues associated with agility of the Agile processes and Scrum frameworks. As it stands, there are a number of scaling agile frameworks and they are designed primarily to address these problems. Some of these scaling frameworks include Nexus, Spotify model, Scrum at Scale, Large-Scale Scrum (LeSS), Scaled Agile Framework (SAFe), and Disciplined Agile, among others. Depending on your choice, each of these frameworks works differently and with a solution in focus.

Scaling Scrum Frameworks

1. Large-Scale Scrum

Large-Scale Scrum is a framework used for multiple teams for scaling agile development and project. Its working is built on a number of principles that provide simple structures, rules and guidelines. The rules focus on adopting Scrum in large product development

The framework works better and is a perfect starting choice for a team that already has a Scrum in place. It is a great scaling framework for small and medium team. So, if you want to scale up with more teams, then choose LeSS. But the scaling has to be one team at a time.

Features of LeSS

- Works on the mechanism of empiricism, self-managing and self-motivating teams, organizational designs, theory of constraints, systems thinking, lean waste, and queuing theory, etc.
- Provides structures and guidelines for adopting Scrum in big product development.
- Scales up with minimal additional process and not single-team Scrum.
- Perfect for small and medium scrum scaling solutions
- Practices setting agenda to achieve Scrum's purpose

2. Scaled Agile Framework (SAFe)

SAFe is an advanced way to scale Scrum. As an interactive knowledge-based framework, SAFe is designed for large organizations. It is meant to execute agile practices at enterprise or large-scale level. The framework is built with a lot of guidance, covering a wide range of areas including financing and enterprise architecture.

SAFe template seeks to solve organization's issues at four (technically three) levels, namely:

- Team level
- Program level
- Large solution level (optional)
- Portfolio level

At the Team scale, SAFe works like Scrum in conjunction with some Extreme Programming practices. At the level of the Programme, SAFe aligns the team around some additional common events to create an Agile Release Train (ART); the Large solution level is the level where SAFe adds some value stream layer. It is introduced to manage large solutions that can't be handled by a single program. Typically, it is hidden to newbies at SAFe. Meanwhile, SAFe links the goal of the organization to ART at the Portfolio level.

Features of SAFe

- Designed for large sized organizations
- Links strategic enterprise goals to Agile Release Train
- Operates at four levels: three essential, one optional
- Comes with a lot of guidance

3. Nexus

Nexus is a scaling framework intended to integrate teams. It is intended for 3 to 9 Scrum teams. In this sense, a typical Scrum Development Team can make up of 3 to 9 members of team. However, there will be more coordination for bigger teams.

As against other scaling frameworks, Nexus aims to resolve the alignment and integration issues through its Nexus Integration Team. The team has its events which prepare for the individual original Scrum events per team. While it takes its primary role of aligning and integrating, the Nexus Integration Team is also responsible for overseeing the following duties and teams:

- **Nexus Planning** — responsible for discussing the overall scope and dependencies. The discussions from here often led to actualization of Nexus Sprint Goal which is closely followed by Scrum Team also organizing its own events with their individual Sprint Goals in line with the Nexus Sprint Goal.
- **Nexus Daily Scrum** — a meeting preceding Scrum Team Daily Scrums where the team addresses issues bothering on alignment and integration
- **A Nexus Review** — replaces the standard Sprint Review(s).
- A Nexus Retrospective— meets prior to the team's Sprint Retrospective to discuss issues relating to Nexus level.

4. Disciplined Agile (DA)

Typically, Disciplined Agile is not designed to be a scaling framework. On the contrary, it is a process decision process model intended to offer a comprehensive guide for an Agile transformation. DA makes use of two of Agile processes including Scrum and Kanban and a host of other transformation knowledge in areas such as Governance, Human Resource and Finance, Portfolio Management and Culture.

As a one stop shop, Disciplined Agile is designed in such a way as to achieve specific goals that allow users to consider their options and learn about their choices. Interestingly, DA is especially attractive for its usefulness because it is designed based on real data. It provides users with an insight into what's going on in other organizations.

As a practice-oriented framework, DA promotes organizational awareness that's based on industry successes, pragmatism, and utility and looks to consider what works and doesn't work in other organization.

Features of DA

- Promotes insight into organizational working and non-functional principles.
- It is a practical framework that operates on the principle of what works and what doesn't work.
- Designed to provide guide for an Agile transformation

- Covers wide range of knowledge based areas like HR, Finance, Portfolio Management, etc.
- Not a scaling framework per se, but a process decision model.

5. **Spotify Engineering Culture**

The Spotify Engineering Culture is a completely different approach. It comes with a bit of oddity as it offers models that the likes of LeSS, Nexus, SAFe and DA do not.

The Spotify Model does not necessarily utilize Scrum. The team within this framework are at liberty to choose which platform they think is suitable for their project. Meaning that they may or may not go for Scrum.

One other feature is that the model focuses on team autonomy rather than alignment. In other words, the model lays emphasis on team's independence and firm coupling of enterprise structure, design and architecture rather than integrating systems. In that way, there is a severe limit to alignment.

Features

- Offers freedom of framework choice for team
- Focuses on organization system and design
- Emphasizes team autonomy rather than alignment
- It is not necessarily a Scrum model

Chapter 14

CONCLUSION

At the introduction, we give you a story of Jakes and how he was able to overcome the initial difficulty he faced while trying to improve the productivity of his team. Little did Jakes and the Board knew that team, quality delivery and assurance, collaboration and built-in quality are the essentials that the company needed to be effective an efficient. The moment he realized the power of Scrum, then he knew his company was in for a real turnaround. Scrum is indeed the way to go.

www.ingramcontent.com/pod-product-compliance
Lightning Source LLC
Chambersburg PA
CBHW070652220526
45466CB00001B/408